NO-FAIL GLUTEN-FREE BREAD BAKING

No-Fail Gluten-Free Bread Baking

*Classic Bread Recipes
for the Texture & Flavor You Love*

PAMELA ELLGEN

ROCKRIDGE
PRESS

Book Design © Jennifer Durrant

Front cover photograph © Marija Vidal 2018; Interior and back cover photography © Melina Thompson 2018; Author photo by Rich Ellgen 2018

Illustrations © Tom Bingham 2018

ISBN: Print 978-1-64152-019-5 | eBook 978-1-64152-020-1

FOR
BRAD & COLE

Contents

Introduction

Few if any other foods hold the cultural significance that bread does. Since the dawn of civilization, humans around the world have ground grains, mixed them with water, and set them by the fire or into an oven to bake. Bread is the staff of life—quite literally for the millions of people who rely on it as their primary source of sustenance.

And yet, for me and so many others with celiac disease, a wheat allergy, or non-celiac gluten sensitivity, the thrill of baking and the pleasure of eating good bread are often a distant memory. Most of us know what it tastes like—or at least what it should taste like—and reminisce about tearing off a hunk of French baguette and dunking it into olive oil or slathering a piece of sourdough toast with butter... sigh.

I went gluten-free nearly a decade ago, when the only options for gluten-free bread were leaden loaves of brown rice bread. They weighed as much as a brick and tasted only slightly better, something like yeast, sand, and sawdust. Initially, I opted for no bread at all. And the sacrifice was worth it. I said goodbye to a lifetime of unexplained stomachaches, mysterious tingling in my arms and legs, nagging food cravings, and mood swings. Eventually I learned to bake without wheat and found gluten-free products that were, well, good enough.

We've come a long way since then. Today you can find gluten-free sandwich breads and ciabatta even in mainstream grocery stores. While these commercial varieties are getting better, and they might answer the daily dilemma of what to pack in your kids' lunchboxes, they don't quite satisfy that longing

for good bread. You know, the kind of bread that stretches gently as you tear it from the loaf. The kind of bread you bite into and savor. The kind of bread that makes wherever you are feel like home.

In *The Art of Eating*, M.F.K. Fisher describes bread making as an almost hypnotic business, "like a dance from some ancient ceremony. It leaves you filled with one of the world's sweetest smells.... There is no chiropractic treatment, no Yoga exercise, no hour of meditation in a music-throbbing chapel that will leave you emptier of bad thoughts than this homely ceremony of making bread."

In this book, I want to connect you with the homely ceremony of making bread, fill your kitchen with the sweetest smells, and leave you eagerly anticipating many future encounters with delicious, homemade, gluten-free bread.

chapter one
Principles of Gluten-Free Bread

Many gluten-free baking books begin by telling you to forget everything you know about baking. But you needn't do that. Yeast is still yeast. It still feasts on starches, converting them to sugar to leaven bread. It still needs time to do its yeasty business. No matter the grains you use, they are still ground to a powder to compose our bread. Some feel like silk between our fingers. Others are nutty and rough. Some of them are ancient. We combine them with other grains to bring out the unique taste and texture we want in each loaf. Like the millennia of bakers who have gone before us, we bake our bread with the precision of a chemist and the artistry of a painter.

How is gluten-free baking so different? It isn't. And this fact shouldn't be forgotten. While gluten-free baking differs in a few consequential ways from baking with wheat flour, which I will hereinafter call "traditional baking," the prevailing principles are the same, and the joy of baking bread belongs to us as well.

Beyond Traditional Baking

Before we explore the nuances of gluten-free baking, let's briefly discuss baking with wheat flour and which characteristics of flour help make really good bread. By understanding traditional baking, we are better equipped to replicate it in our gluten-free baking.

Gluten is a protein found in wheat, barley, rye, and triticale (a hybrid of wheat and rye). Gluten can also be found in other grains, such as oats, due to cross-contamination. When wheat flour is mixed with water, the proteins glutenin and gliadin develop within about seven minutes to form gluten, which gives the dough an elastic quality, especially when fully developed through kneading. This allows the dough to stretch as it rises, giving way to pockets of air without falling apart. Modern, genetically engineered varieties of wheat exploit this quality of gluten, making it even stretchier and stronger—which is in all likelihood more damaging to our gut. In gluten-free baking, this stretchiness is instead achieved through a blend of flours and starches and the addition of emulsifiers and gums.

Wheat flour also has a delicious flavor. In her excellent baking book *Gluten-Free Baking Classics*, Annalise G. Roberts remarks that we never really stop to think about the flavor found in wheat flour until we begin baking without it. Wheat flour is relatively tasteless when raw, but in the hands of a skillful baker, wheat flour can transform into something nutty, caramelized, and rich. In gluten-free baking, this flavor is replicated through other ingredients and techniques. A blend of flours, including at least one nonwheat whole-grain flour, along with a slight increase in sugar, can mimic this flavor. So, too, do fermentation and baking at high temperatures.

Traditional bakers utilize different types of wheat flour with slightly different ratios of gluten to achieve their desired results. Cake and pastry flours contain up to 10 percent gluten, all-purpose flour has roughly 12 percent gluten, and bread flour has between 13 and 14 percent gluten. The yeast breads in this book rely on a gluten-free bread flour blend that uses gluten-free flours to replicate the effects of bread flour's higher gluten content. The quick breads in this book use a gluten-free flour blend more similar to pastry flour or all-purpose flour.

Wheat flour also has a texture that lends itself well to baking. It contributes to a delicate crumb, when that is desired, as well as a crusty exterior, a cool and smooth interior, and a pleasing, chewy texture. But the gluten-free crowd has options, too, thanks to the experimentation of many culinary pros. In gluten-free baking, this texture is achieved through a blend of flours, starches, and gums.

What to Expect

Although gluten-free bread baking bears many similarities to traditional bread baking, there are a couple key differences you should anticipate. Gluten-free flours, especially starches, do not hydrate fully until they're heated. This means that your gluten-free dough will often resemble batter. Resist the temptation to keep adding flour until it looks like traditional bread dough—this will ruin your loaf. You will produce baguettes so hard that they are more useful slathered with mortar than butter!

You can also expect to enjoy your bread a little sooner. Because gluten-free bread dough requires only one rise, and that rise is shorter than it is in traditional baking, you're always just about an hour from a really good loaf of bread.

Finally, raise your expectations—you are going to make really good bread. It will not be exactly identical to the breads made with wheat flour because, plain and simple, it isn't. In his book *The Bread Baker's Apprentice*, a master class in bread making, Peter Reinhart reminds bakers that at the end of the day, you're making homemade bread, and even if it doesn't turn out exactly as you intended, it will be good. Really good.

6 Essential Steps of Gluten-Free Bread Baking

Especially if you're just starting out in gluten-free baking, be sure to follow these essential steps of gluten-free bread baking for excellent results every time.

Step 1: Follow the recipe closely.

Following a baking recipe closely is typically essential to getting the desired results, and this is especially true in gluten-free bread baking.

Each gluten-free flour and gum has unique properties that are harnessed to produce precise results in each recipe. For best results, ingredients should be used in the exact quantities specified. Bread should rise for exactly the time specified at exactly the temperature specified. Unfortunately, this is just not one of those things you can eyeball, like a frittata or a homemade Chex mix. Substitutions, inaccurate measuring, differences in proofing temperature, and all other deviations from recipes will result in something different from what is intended in each recipe. I want your baked product to be as delicious and texturally on point as it can be.

That said, one day you will run out of flours. You will be pressed for time. Or you will just want to try something new. Ignore everything I just said and go for it! As you learn how to manipulate the variables in baking and discover how each gluten-free flour behaves, you will be able to customize recipes to your tastes and preferences. Certainly, the results will be different. They may be worse, but they may be better. That is how good gluten-free bread will continue to evolve for generations to come. Who knows what you may discover?

Step 2: Measure accurately.

Indeed, measuring ingredients accurately matters much more in baking than in other methods of cooking. Once again, this is especially true in gluten-free baking. The difference between ½ teaspoon xanthan gum and 1 teaspoon xanthan gum is the difference between a soft, tender banana bread and a banana gummy bear.

These are the methods I use for measuring ingredients. If you follow the same methods, you will achieve the same results.

To measure flours, sugar, salt, or gum, the best method is to scoop the ingredient out of a larger container with a spoon and lower it into a measuring spoon or dry measuring cup; the vessel should have level edges and no pour spout. Continue scooping the dry ingredient from the larger container into the cup until it is more than full. Use the spoon handle or the back side of a butter knife to scrape excess from the measuring cup, running the utensil along the top edges of the measuring cup. Allow the excess ingredient to fall into the original container or into a separate, clean bowl. Do not tap the measuring cup to settle the ingredient, and don't press the ingredient down with the utensil.

To measure liquid ingredients, use measuring spoons for small amounts. For larger amounts, use a clear glass liquid measuring cup. Pour the liquid into the measuring cup, then set it on a level surface. When it is still, look at it straight on from the side to determine if the liquid line matches the correct measuring line. Pour out excess liquid, or add liquid by the spoonful until it is level.

Many baking books recommend baking by weight instead of using measuring spoons and cups. However, I have found that consistent measuring yields consistent results even without a scale. Logically speaking, for thousands of years bakers have baked really good bread without using a digital scale. In fact, they have produced bread that inspired Janet Flanner to write in *Paris Was Yesterday, 1925–1939*, "In the history of art there are periods when bread seems so beautiful that it nearly gets into museums." Bakers did this without many kitchen implements, including digital scales, and you can, too.

That said, I have found a scale to be especially helpful in measuring grains before grinding. For example, 100 grams of oats yields 1¼ cups of oat flour.

Step 3: Mix mindfully.

Most gluten-free bread doughs do not require kneading with your hands and instead rely on mixing with a stand mixer using the whisk attachment. Most gluten-free doughs resemble cake batter; some are slightly thinner and others are much thicker.

First, you'll want to sift together your dry ingredients. In particular, it is important to disburse any xanthan gum (see page 9) throughout your dry ingredients before adding the wet ingredients.

Next, add the wet ingredients and mix for about 15 seconds. Scrape down the sides of the bowl and then mix again. Most yeast bread recipes call for mixing on medium speed with a whisk or paddle attachment for 3 minutes to activate the xanthan gum. If you don't have a stand mixer, you can use a hand mixer. Without a hand mixer, you can use a wire whisk initially just to combine all of the ingredients completely. This will become tiresome quickly. Switch to a silicone spatula to continue mixing for the remainder of the specified time.

Quick breads call for mixing only until the ingredients are thoroughly combined. If nuts, seeds, or dried fruit are added, they are folded in by hand at the end of the mixing time.

Step 4: Proof with care.

Gluten-free bread doughs need only one rise. Because there's no need to develop and strengthen the gluten bonds—in fact, we don't have the luxury of these bonds to keep the integrity of our loaf—dough should rise for a brief period of time and no longer than specified in each recipe. Some recipes recommend a warm environment for proofing (allowing the dough to rise), about 80°F. Other recipes do better in a room-temperature environment, about 70°F. To illustrate the difference that temperature makes, for every increase of 17°F, rising time is cut in half. For example, a recipe that requires 30 minutes rising time at 70°F could be fully risen in 15 minutes at 87°F. However, cooler temperatures contribute to a more even rise and a more stable bread. Hence, for breads that require more structure, a room-temperature environment will suffice. If your home is much cooler than room temperature, you can heat your oven briefly, then turn it off and leave the light on. Pilot lights inside an oven will usually keep it slightly warmer than room temperature. Use an oven thermometer to confirm the temperature inside your oven.

In most instances, I do not cover dough with plastic wrap while it rises, for a few reasons. First, the dough rises for such a short time, it doesn't dry out very much, and actually, a slight development of a skin on the surface of the dough is a good thing. Second, many gluten-free doughs are so soft and sticky that the plastic wrap would stick to it and create a huge mess. So, no need to waste the plastic.

Bread will continue to rise in the oven while it is baking. This is traditionally called "oven spring." The recipes in this book rely on oven spring to produce the desired rise and volume.

Step 5: Set the correct oven temperature—for sure.

All recipes require placing your bread into a preheated oven. However, when a recipe has a rising time, the instruction to preheat the oven is timed midway through the directions. Resist the urge to bake bread in an oven that is not yet fully preheated.

Oven temperatures can vary considerably. To ensure that your oven heats to the correct temperature, test it out with an oven thermometer. This can also tell you whether the oven is in fact fully preheated when it indicates that it is.

The recipes in this book were tested with a conventional oven. If you have a convection oven, breads will brown and bake more quickly. General recommendations are to begin checking doneness when 75 percent of the baking time has elapsed.

Step 6: Let the bread cool.

Like with all foods, bread continues cooking after it has been removed from the heat source. Resist the temptation to cut into your

steaming-hot bread immediately. This is akin to removing the lid from a pot of rice that is steaming. It will halt the cooking process and your bread will end up gummy. The only exception to this rule is those breads that are designed to be enjoyed warm out of the oven, such as Cinnamon Rolls (page 113).

At every step, have fun!

Yes, there are some rules to ensure good results, but ultimately, bread baking is supposed to be fun. It should be life giving. Give yourself the time and space to enjoy the process, and allow for mistakes. If your bread doesn't turn out exactly the way you want it to the first time, examine ways you can improve it. Until you find your perfect loaf, make bread crumbs or croutons from your flops and keep baking!

Recipe Key

In the recipe chapters, you'll see the following symbols for your convenience.

 Dairy Free

 Egg Free

 Nut Free

 Vegan

chapter two
Ingredients and Equipment

The ingredients and equipment required for gluten-free bread baking differ only slightly from those used for traditional baking. The biggest difference—one you're likely well aware of by now—is that you need more than one kind of flour, and these flours do cost more than all-purpose flour. However, once you make the initial investment of several bags of flour and xanthan gum, it's just a couple bucks here and there to replenish your supply. Most of the equipment you'll need is probably already in your kitchen or can easily be procured online.

Tools of the Trade

I am not a "gadget person" and I will not sell you what you don't need. So, when I call for a piece of equipment, it is because it is absolutely essential and I couldn't find a suitable workaround. Here are the essential and nonessential tools I use to craft delicious gluten-free bread.

Essential Tools

LOAF PAN: Metal, nonstick, 9 inches by 5 inches.

RIMMED BAKING SHEET: Metal pan with edges at least 1 inch tall.

FRENCH BREAD PAN: Metal pan with 3- or 4-inch-wide grooves. May be perforated.

HAMBURGER BUN PAN: Metal, nonstick, with 4-inch indentations for making buns and rolls. Six 4-inch ramekins are an acceptable substitute.

INSTANT-READ DIGITAL THERMOMETER: This tool can help you ensure, for example, that you are warming water to 110°F (not 120°F, which will kill the yeast). It is also useful for confirming the internal temperature of baked loaves to ensure they are fully baked.

PARCHMENT PAPER: Used to prevent dough from sticking to pans, especially when baking loaf breads. Please note that wax paper is not a good substitute.

MIXING BOWLS: Various sizes.

DRY AND LIQUID MEASURING CUPS: Dry cups should have level edges and no pour spouts. Liquid cups should be transparent and have a pour spout.

MEASURING SPOONS: Including ⅛ teaspoon up to 1 tablespoon.

Nonessential Tools

These are not critical to delicious baked items, but they can be helpful for certain preparations.

STAND MIXER: Should include whisk and paddle attachments. A hand mixer is an acceptable substitute.

PIZZA STONE OR STEEL: For cooking pizza and flatbreads when a heated surface is desirable to produce a crisp crust.

SPRINGFORM PAN: A cake pan is an acceptable substitute.

MUFFIN TIN: Can also be used in lieu of a hamburger bun pan for Dinner Rolls (page 24).

POPOVER PAN: For Popovers (page 115).

BRIOCHE PAN: For Brioche (page 103).

OVEN THERMOMETER: Helpful for checking your oven's proofing temperature as well as cooking temperature—many ovens run a little hot or cool.

PASTRY BRUSH: For brushing dough with oil or egg wash.

ROLLING PIN: Used for rolling out croissant dough.

KITCHEN SCALE: For weighing ingredients.

The Gluten-Free Baker's Pantry

When I started baking without wheat flour, I had never heard of many of the existing gluten-free flours or gums, let alone cooked with them. Fortunately, they're easier than ever to find and even easier to work with. They can be found in well-stocked grocery stores, health food stores, or online at Amazon or other sites.

Gluten-Free Flours

Some of the gluten-free baking recipes you'll see online specify brands of gluten-free flours. That is a convenient position for a food blogger with affiliate links to the flour manufacturer, but the truth is, the differences between brands are usually imperceptible. Here is a list of the flours used in this book and a description of their properties:

ALMOND FLOUR: Made from ground blanched almonds, it is naturally grain-free and high in protein, with moderate fiber and a low glycemic index. Almond flour yields a rich, chewy texture. Used in six recipes in this book.

BROWN RICE FLOUR: This whole-grain flour is made from stone-ground brown rice. It contains moderate protein and fiber. It gives volume to baked goods and a grainy texture and flavor. Used in most recipes in this book.

GARBANZO BEAN FLOUR: This naturally grain-free flour is made from garbanzo beans, also known as chickpeas. It has high fiber and high protein, and a subtle but distinct flavor. Used in fewer than five recipes in this book.

MILLET FLOUR: Made from ground millet, this naturally whole-grain flour contains moderate fiber and protein. It produces a fine crumb in baking and has a subtle, pleasant flavor. Used in many recipes in this book.

OAT FLOUR: Made from ground oats, this naturally whole-grain flour is high in fiber and contains moderate protein. Must be labeled *gluten-free* to ensure purity. Yields a chewy texture and toasted flavor to baked goods. Used in fewer than five recipes in this book.

POTATO STARCH: Made from high-starch potatoes, this starch is naturally grain-free. Potato starch should not be confused with potato flour. Potato starch has no fiber and no protein and has a high glycemic index. It produces a tender, fine crumb in baking. Used in most recipes in this book.

SORGHUM FLOUR: Made from ground sorghum grain (a whole grain with moderate fiber and protein), it possesses a neutral flavor. Used in many recipes in this book.

SWEET RICE FLOUR: This flour, also called mochi flour, is made from glutinous rice but contains no gluten. Its thickening properties yield a chewy texture, and it has a neutral flavor. Used in many recipes in this book.

TAPIOCA FLOUR/STARCH: Made from cassava root, this flour is naturally grain-free. It has a high glycemic index and no fiber or protein. It has thickening and gelling properties. Used in most recipes in this book.

XANTHAN GUM: This fine polysaccharide powder is derived from fermentation. It is used in very small quantities to mimic the elastic qualities of gluten and to allow foods to rise properly. If used in excess, it can produce a gummy texture. A bag is expensive (more than $12 for an 8-ounce bag as of the printing of this book) but will last years. Used in most recipes in this book.

Water

Filtered water is best, because chlorine can interact with the development of the yeast and enzymes. However, tap water is acceptable.

Salt

Fine sea salt was used to test all of the recipes in this book. If you use table salt, reduce the salt called for by 25 percent. One other caveat: Do not combine salt and yeast by themselves when proofing yeast, because salt will prevent the yeast from digesting the sugars, which will result in an insufficient rise.

Gluten-Free Flour Blends

Many of the recipes in this book use a flour blend. You can mix these ahead of time so you always have them on hand.

WHITE BREAD FLOUR BLEND

(Makes 4 cups)

This flour blend is designed to mimic the taste and texture of bread flour and is used in many of the yeast breads in this book. Like bread flour, it contains relatively little fiber and protein, meaning it isn't a health food per se, but it can be enjoyed as part of a healthy diet. Do not use the bread flour in the quick bread recipes.

1½ cups potato starch

1 cup brown rice flour

1 cup tapioca starch

½ cup sweet rice flour

MULTIGRAIN FLOUR BLEND

(Makes 4¼ cups)

This flour blend is used in many of the multigrain recipes in this book and is adapted from the flour blend I developed for my book *The Gluten-Free Cookbook for Families*.

1 cup millet flour

1 cup sorghum flour

1 cup brown rice flour

¾ cup potato starch

½ cup tapioca starch

OAT FLOUR BLEND

(Makes 4½ cups)

Some individuals are sensitive even to gluten-free oats, so I use this flour blend sparingly in this book. Nevertheless, it is delicious and can be used interchangeably with the preceding Multigrain Flour Blend.

1¼ cups finely ground gluten-free oat flour

1 cup millet flour

1 cup sorghum flour

¾ cup tapioca starch

½ cup potato starch

NOTE: You can also purchase one of the dozens of premade flour blends available, which contain very different ingredients. These alternative flour blends may or may not work in the recipes in this book. If you choose to swap my flour blends for a blend containing different ingredients in different ratios, I can't guarantee your results. The recipes in this book were tested with successful results using the exact flours that I recommend in each recipe.

Eggs

Large, cage-free eggs were used in testing the recipes. Any large egg will do, but eggs should be at room temperature. You can quickly bring eggs to room temperature by placing them in a warm water bath for 15 minutes.

Leaveners and Binders

Active dry yeast was used in testing the recipes that contain yeast. It is not necessary to proof (or prove) yeast by placing it in water before mixing it into the dough unless otherwise noted in a recipe. Instant yeast contains smaller granules of yeast and will leaven baked goods more quickly. If that is what you have available, you can use it, but you will need to reduce the rising time slightly; just follow the visual cues in each recipe (for example, "until doubled" or "until it rises by 50 percent").

Yeast should be stored in a cool, dark place and not exposed to air. Wait to open small yeast packages until you're ready to use them. Keep yeast separate from other ingredients until you are ready to bake (for example, don't mix a pizza crust mix with the yeast until you intend to bake, or it will not leaven properly).

Double-acting, aluminum-free, gluten-free baking powder was used to test all of the recipes in this book that contain baking powder. Because more of this ingredient is used in gluten-free baking than in traditional baking, it is essential to choose a product that does not contain aluminum, which would negatively affect the flavor. Double-acting baking powder means that it begins to work when mixed with liquid and has a second reaction when exposed to heat. Sometimes, baking powder is added to yeast breads to enhance the rise when it is especially useful.

Any baking soda will work in the recipes in this book.

Xanthan gum is the only commercial gum I used when testing the recipes. I have used guar gum in the past, but I prefer the way xanthan gum thickens gluten-free dough before it bakes.

Sugars and Sweeteners

I use white and brown sugar for sweetening dough and feeding the yeast in the recipes in this book. Although yeast cannot immediately digest sucrose (table sugar), it contains the enzymes necessary to convert it to usable glucose. Brown sugar is slightly acidic, which activates baking soda and baking powder. It also contributes a more complex, rich taste.

None of the recipes were tested using alternative sweeteners such as honey, maple syrup, or agave. You can use these in a pinch, but the results will differ. Also, avoid non-nutritive sweeteners such as aspartame, sugar alcohols, or stevia—they will not feed the yeast at all.

Butter and Oils

Canola oil and olive oil are used throughout this book. Vegetable oil is an acceptable substitute.

Unsalted butter and nondairy butter substitutes, such as Earth Balance Buttery Spread, can be used interchangeably throughout the recipes in this book, except in the croissant and shortbread recipes, where the butter characterizes the recipe.

I do not use shortening in this book, but if you choose to use it, a nonhydrogenated palm shortening is the best option for gluten-free baking.

Seeds and Nuts

I utilize a variety of seeds and nuts in this book. Toasting your own nuts and seeds yields the best flavor, but you can also purchase toasted almonds and hazelnuts that will work well.

chapter three
Troubleshooting

Baking requires scientific precision, but even the most careful baker can run into challenges—sunken loaves, bread that won't rise, and baguettes as hard as baseball bats. Even in traditional baking, glitches are bound to occur. While it is not more difficult, gluten-free baking has its own unique set of challenges. Some of those challenges are related solely to expectations of what bread dough "should" look like. Here are a few common situations in gluten-free baking and how to resolve them.

The bread is hard and heavy.

This is probably the most common problem in gluten-free baking. If you're expecting knead-able dough that bounces back when you touch it, you may be tempted to add more and more gluten-free flour to your bowl until the dough resembles wheat-based dough. Doing this virtually guarantees you'll end up with a brick. Resist the urge to add more flour! Also, if you measure flour by dipping a measuring cup into the flour or pack flour into the cup by tapping it on the counter, you will inadvertently add more flour than is called for. Follow the instructions in chapter 1 to ensure accurate measurements.

The bread is gummy and wet.

On the opposite end of the spectrum, gummy, wet bread can occur for a couple of reasons. One reason is the addition of too much xanthan gum. Using more tapioca starch or sweet rice flour than is called for in the recipe can also yield a gummy texture. Xanthan gum is one of the ingredients designed to mimic gluten. Traditional yeast breads often call for bread flour, which contains slightly more gluten than all-purpose flour. In gluten-free baking, more xanthan gum is used when making yeast bread, whereas less gum is used for making quick breads and other gluten-free baked goods. That said, if the dough appears too runny when mixing, it could be that you forgot to add the xanthan gum. I experienced this while mixing dough. It looked too thin for pancake batter until I remembered to add the

xanthan gum. Suddenly the dough thickened, and it was the texture I had come to expect from gluten-free dough.

Another reason for overly wet dough is the addition of wet ingredients, such as shredded carrots, mashed banana, or pumpkin purée, without adjusting the rest of the liquid in the recipe. The most obvious reason for gummy, wet dough, generally, is that too much liquid was used in the recipe.

The bread has a thick, rubbery layer at the bottom.

Similar to the previous problem, this is another very common problem in gluten-free baking, and it, too, may occur for a couple reasons. First, it could be that your dough was too wet. Although gluten-free doughs should be far wetter than wheat dough, too much of anything can wreck the bread. It bears repeating: Follow the recipe for the best results.

Another reason for a gummy layer at the bottom of the bread is that the bread was removed from the oven before it had fully baked. Ovens have varying temperatures, and other factors, such as weather and the tempera-ture of the ingredients in the dough, can affect how quickly bread will bake. Hence, I will indicate a range of time in most recipes. Especially with loaf breads and baguettes, I recommend using an instant-read thermometer to confirm that your loaf has reached an internal temperature of 205°F to 210°F. Insert the thermometer nearly to the bottom of the loaf, without touching the pan with the thermometer.

At-a-Glance Troubleshooting Guide

Issue	*Likely Problem*	*Possible Fix*
Bread is too hard and heavy.	Too much flour	Next time, make sure to measure accurately and/or decrease flour by 2 tablespoons or increase liquid by 1 tablespoon.
Bread is gummy and wet.	Too much xanthan or guar gum; too much tapioca starch or sweet rice flour; or the inclusion of too many wet ingredients	Decrease oven temperature and increase baking time; or next time, measure accurately.
Bread has a rubbery bottom layer.	Dough is too wet or bread removed too early from oven.	Insert a bread thermometer near the bottom to confirm it has reached 205°F to 210°F.
Quick bread texture is wrong.	Flour substitution	In next batch, follow the instructions exactly and use the specified flours.
Yeast bread won't rise.	Bad yeast or liquid too hot and killed yeast	Next time, proof the yeast before adding to recipe and ensure liquid is no more than 110°F.
Bread sinks after cooling.	Bread rose in too warm an environment; dough has too much liquid	Next time, make sure the environment is not over 80°F or humid.
There's a gap between the top of the loaf and the rest of the bread.	Oven rack set too high	Next time, bake in the middle of the oven.

Quick bread has the wrong texture.

There are few, if any, gluten-free flours that can mimic the taste and texture of all-purpose flour. Substituting one or more flours beyond those called for in the recipe can yield dramatically different textures that what is promised in the recipe. If you are new to gluten-free baking, I definitely advise following the recipes exactly as written. If you are converting a wheat recipe to gluten-free, I recommend that you use a premixed flour blend. Cup4Cup and Bob's Red Mill 1-to-1 Baking Flour are two good options.

The yeast bread won't rise.

The most likely culprit for a nonrising bread is that the yeast is bad. One way to solve this is to proof the yeast before adding it to the recipe. Do this by mixing the warmed water (or whatever liquid is called for in the recipe) along with the sugar and yeast. Allow it to sit for 10 minutes. It should become quite foamy. If not, the yeast is bad. Simply purchase a new package and try again.

The bread rose in the oven, then sank after cooling.

This can occur for a few reasons. One reason is that the bread rose too quickly or was allowed to rise too much, which may occur if the bread is allowed to rise in too warm an environment, over 80°F. Another reason is that the bread dough contained too much liquid, which can occur because of overpouring or even something as simple as a very humid day.

There is a large gap between the top of the loaf and the rest of the bread.

This occurs when the bread is baked on an oven rack that's set too high, where the heat is more intense. To ensure an even temperature, always bake in the middle of the oven unless directed otherwise.

FAQs

Can I use egg substitutes?

Yes, egg substitutes will work in many of the recipes, particularly those calling for two or fewer eggs. The best substitute is a commercial egg substitute or aquafaba, the brine from canned chickpeas. Other options, such as chia seeds, flaxseed, and mashed banana, are less reliable.

Can I use dairy substitutes?

Yes. In fact, because many people who cannot eat gluten also cannot consume dairy, most recipes were tested using water or a nondairy milk and nondairy butter.

Can I swap one flour for another?

Occasionally you may run out of one gluten-free flour and need to substitute with another flour. In general, it's best to substitute flours with like flours. For example, if you need to substitute for a starch in a recipe, use another starch. If you need to substitute for a whole-grain flour in a recipe, use another whole-grain flour. If a recipe calls for brown rice flour, white rice flour (but not sweet rice flour) is an acceptable substitute. Swaps work best when the flour being replaced composes only a small portion of the flour in a recipe. That said, the results can't be guaranteed if you swap flours.

WHOLE-GRAIN FLOURS: Brown rice flour, millet flour, amaranth flour, sorghum flour, buckwheat flour

STARCHES: Arrowroot starch, cornstarch, tapioca starch, potato starch

Can I use guar gum instead of xanthan gum?

Yes, guar gum may work in many recipes; however, these recipes were tested using xanthan gum. Guar gum does not thicken the same way xanthan gum does—guar gum thickens with heat, but it does not thicken the batter. Xanthan gum thickens the dough immediately.

How do you store gluten-free bread?

All homemade breads, whether or not gluten-free, have a shorter shelf life than commercial breads. They are usually best on the first day. However, if you have bread that you do not finish immediately, allow it to cool completely and store in a sealed container, such as a zip-top plastic bag, in the refrigerator for up to 3 days. Bread can also be stored in the same manner in the freezer for up to 1 month. It will be edible if stored for longer, but the quality will deteriorate. I recommend slicing bread before freezing it so you can remove just what you need.

High-Altitude Baking

The same principles that apply to traditional high-altitude baking also apply to high-altitude gluten-free baking. If you live above 3,500 feet, you'll want to adapt the recipes in this book accordingly:

- **Increase the baking temperature** by 25°F.

- In quick breads, **decrease the baking powder or baking soda** by about ⅛ teaspoon for every full teaspoon called for.

- In yeast breads, **reduce the proofing time**, observing the appearance of the dough, not the time specified in the recipe.

- For quick breads that call for sugar, **decrease the sugar** by 1 to 3 tablespoons per cup called for in the recipe, depending on your elevation (reduce further at higher elevations).

- **Increase liquids** by 2 to 4 tablespoons per cup called for in the recipe, depending on your elevation (increase further at higher elevations).

- Be sure to **use parchment paper liners or grease your pans** to prevent breads from sticking to the pans.

chapter four
First Loaves

Are your hands covered with flour and ready to get baking some bread? Let's get started! I'd like to begin by sharing five simple recipes that will introduce you to the fundamentals of bread baking. The following tutorials offer detailed information on how to prepare and bake five essential gluten-free breads: Classic Sandwich Bread, French Baguette, Dinner Rolls, Artisan Pizza Crust, and quick bread—specifically, Banana Bread. We'll round out this tutorial section with a how-to for sourdough starter, which is used in several recipes.

BANANA BREAD, PAGE 28

RECIPE TUTORIAL *classic sandwich bread*

PREP TIME: 10 minutes, plus 40 minutes to rise • **COOK TIME:** 55 minutes

Kids are the toughest critics, so when I set about creating a classic sandwich bread that they would love, I knew it would have to be good. This one exceeded my wildest expectations—and theirs! It's chewy, soft, and pillowy with a delicious crackly crust. The baking powder offers an added leavening boost to this sandwich bread. For best results, make sure to use double-acting, aluminum-free— and of course, gluten-free—baking powder.

MAKES 1 LOAF

TOOLS

- Instant-read digital thermometer
- Stand mixer (optional)
- 9-by-5-inch loaf pan
- Parchment paper

3 cups White Bread Flour Blend (page 10)

3 tablespoons sugar

1 (¼-ounce) packet active dry yeast

1 tablespoon double-acting, aluminum-free, gluten-free baking powder

1½ teaspoons xanthan gum

1 teaspoon sea salt

1½ cups water, milk, or nondairy milk

1½ teaspoons apple cider vinegar

3 tablespoons canola oil

2 eggs

Prepare the ingredients

1. Bring the liquid ingredients and eggs to room temperature (see Ingredient tip).

2. Measure the dry ingredients carefully. Shake the covered flour container to aerate it. Use a spoon to scoop flour into a dry measuring cup without a pour spout. Do not tap or shake the measuring cup to settle the contents. Use the spoon handle to level the top, discarding the excess flour into the original container.

3. Using an instant-read digital thermometer to test, warm the water or milk to at least 110°F but not more than 120°F, which would kill the yeast.

Mix the ingredients

1. Place the flour blend, sugar, yeast, baking powder, xanthan gum, and salt into the bowl of a stand mixer or a large mixing bowl. Whisk with the whisk attachment or by hand to combine the ingredients.

2. Add the warmed water or milk, vinegar, oil, and eggs, and mix for 15 seconds.

3. Mix the batter on medium speed for 3 minutes, scraping down the sides of the bowl with a spatula as necessary. It will resemble cake batter.

Proof the dough

1. Preheat the oven to 300°F for 1 minute, just to warm the oven to about 80°F. Turn off the heat.

2. Line the interior of a loaf pan with parchment paper.

3. Pour the batter into the prepared loaf pan. Smooth the top of the batter with a clean spatula, mounding it slightly in the center.

4. Place the pan into the warm oven and let the batter rise for 30 minutes, until nearly doubled in size (see Troubleshooting tip). It should not crest the sides of the pan.

5. Remove the pan from the oven to continue proofing for 10 minutes.

Bake the bread

1. Preheat the oven to 375°F.

2. Place the loaf pan on the center rack and bake for 55 minutes. Bread should have a hollow sound when tapped. Allow to cool for 2 minutes, then run a knife along the sides of the pan and invert the bread on its side on a cooling rack. Allow the bread to cool completely before slicing or storing.

3. Store in a tightly sealed zip-top bag in the refrigerator for up to 3 days.

INGREDIENT TIP: Bringing all ingredients to room temperature will prevent cold eggs, for example, from reducing the temperature of the batter and slowing the rise of the bread.

TROUBLESHOOTING TIP: Do not let the bread proof for too long or it will fall during and after baking.

RECITPE TUTORIAL *french baguette*

PREP TIME: 15 minutes, plus 40 minutes to rise • **COOK TIME:** 35 minutes

Crafting a French bread that lived up to my expectations was my holy grail of gluten-free baking. I didn't want something that was "good for gluten-free" but something that was just plain *good*. As I tested and retested recipes, tinkering with flour ratios and adjusting other variables, a line from the movie *Ratatouille* played in my mind: "How can you tell how good bread is without tasting it? Not the smell, not the look, but the sound of the crust. Listen. Oh, symphony of crackle." When I discovered that symphony, I knew I had created a good bread.

MAKES 2 LOAVES

TOOLS

- French bread pan, perforated is okay
- Parchment paper
- Instant-read digital thermometer
- Baking dish

2 cups plus 2 tablespoons White Bread Flour Blend (page 10)

1 tablespoon sugar

1 (¼-ounce) packet active dry yeast

1 teaspoon xanthan gum

1 teaspoon sea salt

1 cup plus 1 tablespoon water

½ tablespoon canola oil

1 teaspoon potato starch

Prepare the ingredients

1. Bring all the ingredients to room temperature.

2. Line a French bread pan with parchment paper.

3. Measure the dry ingredients carefully. Use a spoon to scoop flour into a dry measuring cup without a pour spout. Do not tap or shake to settle the contents. Use the spoon handle to level the top of the measuring cup, discarding excess flour into the original container.

4. Using an instant-read digital thermometer to test, warm the water to at least 110°F but not more than 120°F, which would kill the yeast.

Mix the ingredients

1. In a medium bowl, sift the flour blend, sugar, yeast, xanthan gum, and salt. Set aside.

2. Add the water and oil to the bowl, and mix for 30 seconds. Scrape down the sides of the bowl, and mix for 3 additional minutes.

Proof the dough

1. Spoon the batter into the prepared French bread pan to form 2 baguettes about 12 inches long. Smooth the top of the batter with a clean spatula, without flattening it.

2. Sift the potato starch over the bread dough and pat gently with your hands to smooth the tops.

3. Let the dough rise at room temperature for 40 minutes, or until it has nearly doubled in size (see Troubleshooting tip).

Bake the baguettes

1. Preheat the oven to 400°F. Place a baking dish filled with at least 2 cups of hot water on the bottom rack of the oven.

2. Place the bread pan on the center rack, and bake for 35 minutes. It should have a hollow sound when tapped and be slightly golden brown on the top. Allow the bread to cool completely before slicing.

3. Serve or store up to 3 days in a zip-top bag in the refrigerator.

BAKING TIP: The French baguette does not respond well to scoring, because it is not stiff enough and the cuts will not remain after the dough has risen.

TROUBLESHOOTING TIP: Don't let the dough proof too long or it will fall during and after baking.

PREP TIME: 10 minutes, plus 45 minutes to rise • **COOK TIME:** 20 minutes

Soft, pillowy dinner rolls are essential to holiday tables, and I resigned myself to years of "going without" before discovering this delicious recipe. Here's how to master them.

MAKES 8 ROLLS

TOOLS

- Instant-read digital thermometer
- Stand mixer (optional)
- 8-inch round cake pan
- Parchment paper

2 cups White Bread Flour Blend (page 10)

1 tablespoon sugar

1 (¼-ounce) packet active dry yeast

1½ teaspoons xanthan gum

1 teaspoon sea salt

½ cup milk or nondairy milk

1 egg

3 tablespoons butter or nondairy butter

Prepare the ingredients

1. Bring all the ingredients to room temperature. Line a cake pan with parchment paper.

2. Measure the dry ingredients carefully. Use a spoon to scoop the flour into a dry measuring cup without a pour spout. Do not tap or shake to settle the contents. Use the spoon handle to level the top, discarding excess flour into the original container.

3. Using an instant-read digital thermometer to test, warm the milk to at least 110°F but not more than 120°F, which would kill the yeast.

Mix the ingredients

1. In a large mixing bowl or the bowl of a stand mixer, whisk together the flour blend, sugar, yeast, xanthan gum, and salt.

2. Add the milk, egg, and butter to the bowl and mix until thoroughly integrated and smooth, scraping down the sides of the bowl as necessary.

Figure A

Figure B

Proof the dough

1. Preheat the oven to 300°F for 1 minute, just to warm the oven to about 80°F. Turn off the heat.

2. Divide the dough mixture into 8 portions and shape them into balls (figure A) (see Troubleshooting tip).

3. Place the dough balls in the prepared pan.

4. Place the pan in the warm oven and let the dough rise for 45 minutes, until doubled in size (figure B). Remove from the oven.

Bake the rolls

1. Preheat the oven to 400°F.

2. Place the pan on the center rack and bake for 20 minutes. Allow the rolls to cool briefly before serving.

3. Store in a zip-top bag in the refrigerator.

TROUBLESHOOTING TIP: Dust your hands with a gluten-free starchy flour, such as potato starch or arrowroot, before shaping the dough, to keep it from sticking to your hands.

RECILE TUTORIAL *artisan pizza crust*

PREP TIME: 10 minutes, plus 30 minutes to rise • **COOK TIME:** 20 minutes

While I was working on this book, I had to evacuate Santa Barbara due to a wildfire and ended up spending a week living with friends out of state. During the time away, my son Brad insisted we try a different pizza place every night (okay, not *every* night), and I ended up trying several different gluten-free crusts from restaurants specializing in wood-fired pizza. This pizza journey proved to be a blessing in disguise (okay, pizza is always a blessing) as I honed exactly what I'm looking for in a good gluten-free crust. I want it to be sturdy enough to pick up but also tender, chewy, golden, and crusty on the bottom. Not at all like a cracker. This crust has it all. It is now my go-to crust for family pizza nights.

YIELDS 2 (12-INCH) CRUSTS
OR 4 (8-INCH) CRUSTS

TOOLS

- Instant-read digital thermometer
- 2 pizza pans
- 2 pizza stones (optional)
- Parchment paper

½ cup brown rice flour

½ cup sweet rice flour

½ cup potato starch

1 tablespoon sugar

1 (¼-ounce) packet active dry yeast

1 teaspoon sea salt

½ teaspoon xanthan gum

¾ cup plus 2 tablespoons water

1 teaspoon extra-virgin olive oil

Prepare the ingredients

1. Measure the dry ingredients carefully. Use a spoon to scoop flour into a dry measuring cup without a pour spout. Do not tap or shake the measuring cup to settle the contents. Use the spoon handle to level the top, discarding excess flour into the original container.

2. Using an instant-read digital thermometer to test, warm the water to at least 110°F but not more than 120°F, which would kill the yeast.

Mix the ingredients

1. In a large bowl, combine the brown rice flour, sweet rice flour, potato starch, sugar, yeast, salt, and xanthan gum.

2. Add the water and oil to the bowl, and mix for 15 seconds. Scrape down the sides of the bowl with a spatula. Mix for 3 additional minutes.

Proof the dough

1. Preheat the oven to 300°F for 1 minute, until it reaches a temperature of 80°F. Turn off the oven.

2. Cut 2 or 4 squares of parchment paper, depending on how many crusts you plan to make. Place them on 2 pizza pans.

3. Divide the dough into 2 or 4 pieces. Use a spatula to spread the dough onto each square of parchment paper in a very thin layer. The dough will have the consistency of frosting and should be spread about as thinly. It will thicken slightly during rising and baking.

4. Place the pans in the oven and allow the dough to rise for 30 minutes. Remove the pans from the oven.

Bake the crust

1. Preheat the oven to 400°F. If using pizza stones, place them on the center rack while the oven is preheating (see Baking tip).

2. Place the pizza pans in the oven, or slide the pizza dough and parchment from the pans onto the preheated pizza stones.

3. Bake for 10 minutes (shorter for a thinner crust), then top with whatever toppings you like and bake for another 10 minutes.

INGREDIENT TIP: Resist the urge to swap out any of the flours called for. Each one is essential, and results will vary wildly (trust me) if you use any different flours.

BAKING TIP: Preheated baking stones work best for baking crusts. However, if you don't have baking stones, pizza pans or baking sheets will do—just don't preheat them; they can warp.

RECICE TUTORIAL *banana bread*

PREP TIME: 10 minutes • **COOK TIME:** 45 to 50 minutes

Fragrant lemon zest and vanilla extract permeate this delectable banana bread, which exists on this ethereal plane between bread and dessert. It is equally at home with coffee at the breakfast table, gently warmed for afternoon tea, or studded with dark chocolate for a most satisfying after-dinner treat.

MAKES 1 LOAF

TOOLS

- 9-by-5-inch loaf pan
- Parchment paper

8 tablespoons (1 stick) butter or nondairy butter, at room temperature

½ cup brown sugar

Zest of 1 lemon

1 teaspoon vanilla extract

2 eggs

1¼ cups mashed bananas

1½ cups Multigrain Flour Blend (page 10)

2 teaspoons double-acting, aluminum-free, gluten-free baking powder

½ teaspoon xanthan gum

½ teaspoon sea salt

½ cup chopped toasted pecans (optional)

½ cup chopped chocolate pieces (optional)

Prepare the ingredients

1. Preheat the oven to 350°F. Line a loaf pan with parchment paper.

2. Measure the dry ingredients carefully. Use a spoon to scoop flour into a dry measuring cup without a pour spout. Do not tap or shake the measuring cup to settle the contents. Use the spoon handle to level the top of the measuring cup, discarding excess flour into the original container.

Mix the ingredients

1. In a large bowl, cream the butter and sugar, beating until light and fluffy, about 1 minute.

2. Add the lemon zest, vanilla, and eggs. Beat until thoroughly mixed, about 30 seconds.

3. Add the mashed bananas and mix until just integrated.

4. In a separate bowl, sift the flour blend, baking powder, xanthan gum, and salt. Add the flour mixture to the butter-egg mixture, and mix until just blended.

5. Fold in the pecans and chocolate pieces, if using.

Bake the bread

1. Pour the mixture into the prepared pan. Some of the leavening agents in quick breads begin working immediately when mixed with water, so do not allow the batter to sit for more than a few minutes before placing it in the oven.

2. Bake for 45 to 50 minutes, until a wooden skewer inserted in the center of the loaf comes out clean. If circulation is poor in your oven, you can rotate the pan after the quick bread has risen and at least two-thirds of the baking time has elapsed. Any sooner will introduce cool air to the oven and hinder the bread from rising properly.

INGREDIENT TIP: Use very ripe bananas in this recipe for the best flavor and texture.

A Note on Quick Breads

Unlike the four previous recipes, this banana bread is a quick bread, meaning it does not use yeast as a leavening agent. The leavening of quick breads is instead generated by baking soda or baking powder (sometimes a combination of both) and eggs. Baking gluten-free quick breads, such as muffins, biscuits, scones, and this banana bread, is similar to traditional baking with wheat. Although the batter will be slightly thinner, it is not as stark a contrast as the difference observed with yeast breads.

Sourdough Starter

Sourdough bread is the most time-consuming of all the recipes in this book, because it requires a starter. Nevertheless, it is easy, and most of the time is not active. You'll want to begin this process at least one week before you intend to bake sourdough bread.

WHAT IS A STARTER?

Sourdough starter is a combination of water and flour that contains wild yeasts and bacteria that work to leaven the bread. In traditional baking, you can make the starter yourself or obtain an established starter from a friend. However, in gluten-free baking, you will have better results if you purchase a small packet of sourdough starter and mix it with water and gluten-free flour to activate. Gluten-free sourdough starters are available online from companies such as Cultures for Health and King Arthur Flour. Each brand of gluten-free starter has its own set of instructions for activating the starter.

The following instructions work with the Cultures for Health Gluten-Free Sourdough Starter. If you choose to use another starter, such as Florapan, follow the instructions provided to activate that starter. Other gluten-free sourdough starters will also work in the sourdough bread recipes in this book.

ACTIVATE THE STARTER

¼ teaspoon Cultures for Health Gluten-Free Sourdough Starter

4 to 8 cups brown rice flour, divided

4 to 8 cups filtered water, divided, at room temperature

1. In a 1-quart glass jar, combine the sourdough starter, 1 tablespoon of brown rice flour, and 1 tablespoon of room-temperature water. Stir with a nonreactive spoon or whisk. Cover the top of the jar with a coffee filter fitted with a rubber band. Set aside for 6 hours.

2. Feed the starter by adding 2 tablespoons of brown rice flour and 2 tablespoons of water. Stir to mix thoroughly. Set aside for 6 hours.

3. Feed the starter by adding ¼ cup of brown rice flour and ¼ cup of water. Stir to mix thoroughly. Set aside for 6 hours.

4. Feed the starter by adding ½ cup of brown rice flour and ½ cup of water. Stir to mix thoroughly. Set aside for 6 hours. This mixture is hereinafter referred to as"the starter."

5. Discard all but ½ cup of the starter and feed the remaining starter by adding ½ cup brown rice flour and ½ cup water.

6. Repeat step 5 every 6 hours (twice daily) for 3 to 7 days, or until the starter has the consistency of pancake batter and bubbles within a few hours of feeding.

To store the starter, keep it in the refrigerator and repeat step 5 every 3 or 4 days.

To use the starter immediately, continue feeding but do not discard any of the starter until it has reached 1 cup in total volume. Use ½ cup of the starter in your first loaf. Skip the "Prepare the starter for baking" section below and go straight to the recipe instructions.

PREPARE THE STARTER FOR BAKING

1. If you have kept the starter in the refrigerator, 8 to 12 hours before you plan to make the sourdough bread, place the jar containing the sourdough starter on the counter and feed it with ¼ cup water and ¼ cup brown rice flour at 4- to 6-hour intervals. Stir and cover the jar with a coffee filter. Allow to sit at room temperature for 8 to 12 hours.

2. Remove the amount of prepared starter that is required for the recipe, and return the rest of the master sourdough starter to the refrigerator. Use the starter as directed.

chapter five
Sandwich Breads

hearty multigrain bread

PREP TIME: 10 minutes, plus 40 minutes to rise • **COOK TIME:** 55 minutes

I grew up enjoying multigrain bread, which made the bland, starchy, gluten-free breads available in the store even more disappointing when I went gluten-free nearly a decade ago. This hearty loaf satisfies my cravings and is loaded with nutrition!

MAKES 1 LOAF

TOOLS

- 9-by-5-inch loaf pan
- Parchment paper
- Stand mixer (optional)

3 cups Multigrain Flour Blend (page 10)

3 tablespoons brown sugar

1 tablespoon double-acting, aluminum-free, gluten-free baking powder

1 (¼-ounce) packet active dry yeast

1½ teaspoons xanthan gum

1 teaspoon sea salt

1½ cups water, milk, or nondairy milk, warmed to 110°F

2 eggs, at room temperature

3 tablespoons canola oil

1½ teaspoons apple cider vinegar

1 tablespoon gluten-free oats (optional)

1. Preheat the oven at 300°F for about 1 minute, until it reaches a temperature of 80°F. Turn off the heat.

2. Line a loaf pan with parchment paper.

3. Place the flour blend, brown sugar, baking powder, yeast, xanthan gum, and salt into the bowl of a stand mixer or a large bowl. Mix for a few seconds to blend the dry ingredients.

4. Add the water, eggs, oil, and cider vinegar, and mix for 15 seconds. Scrape down the sides of the bowl with a spatula, and mix on medium speed for 3 minutes (see Baking tip).

5. Pour the batter into the prepared pan. Sprinkle with the oats (if using).

6. Place the pan in the oven and allow the batter to rise for 30 minutes. It should not crest the sides of the pan.

7. Remove the pan from the oven. Preheat the oven to 375°F while the batter continues to rise at room temperature for 10 more minutes.

8. Bake for 55 minutes. Remove the pan from the oven, and allow to rest for 2 minutes. Run a knife along the sides of the pan, and invert it onto a cooling rack. Allow the bread to cool on its side completely before slicing.

9. Serve or store in a tightly sealed zip-top bag in the refrigerator for up to 3 days.

BAKING TIP: The batter will be runnier than expected—slightly thicker than cake batter.

sourdough sandwich bread

PREP TIME: 10 minutes, plus 8 to 12 hours to prepare the starter and 4 hours to rise
COOK TIME: 45 minutes

As a child, when I visited my grandmother, we would always eat sourdough toast with peanut butter for breakfast. To this day, whenever I think about sourdough, my first tastes of the tangy bread come to mind. Whatever your first memories of sourdough bread are, this sandwich bread will take you right back. Like all breads in this chapter, it's delicious toasted, too.

MAKES 1 LOAF

TOOLS

- 9-by-5-inch loaf pan
- Parchment paper
- Stand mixer (optional)

For the starter

½ cup Sourdough Starter (page 30)

½ cup brown rice flour

½ cup filtered water

For the bread

3 cups White Bread Flour Blend (page 10)

3 tablespoons sugar

1 tablespoon double-acting, aluminum-free, gluten-free baking powder

1½ teaspoons xanthan gum

1 teaspoon sea salt

½ cup Sourdough Starter

3 tablespoons canola oil

1 cup water, warmed to 110°F

2 eggs, at room temperature

To prepare the starter

1. Eight to 12 hours before you plan to make the sourdough bread, place the jar containing the sourdough starter (prepared according to the master tutorial instructions on page 30) on the counter and feed it with ¼ cup water and ¼ cup brown rice flour at 4- to 6-hour intervals. Stir and cover the jar with a coffee filter. Allow to sit at room temperature for 8 to 12 hours.

2. Remove ½ cup of prepared starter that is required for this recipe, and return the rest of the master sourdough starter to the refrigerator.

To make the bread

1. Preheat the oven to 300°F for about 1 minute, until it reaches 80°F. Turn off the heat, but turn on the oven light to generate a slight amount of heat.

2. Line a loaf pan with parchment paper.

3. Place the flour blend, sugar, baking powder, xanthan gum, and salt into the bowl of a stand mixer or a large bowl. Mix just to combine the dry ingredients.

4. Add the sourdough starter, oil, water, and eggs to the bowl, and mix for 15 seconds. Scrape down the sides of the bowl with a spatula, and mix on medium speed for 3 minutes.

CONTINUED ►

5. Pour the batter into the prepared pan (see Baking tip).

6. Place the pan in the oven and allow the batter to rise for 4 hours.

7. Remove the pan from the oven, then preheat the oven to 375°F.

8. Bake for 45 minutes. Remove the pan from the oven and allow to rest for 2 minutes. Run a knife along the sides of the pan, and invert it onto a cooling rack. Allow the bread to cool on its side completely before slicing.

9. Serve or store in a tightly sealed zip-top bag in the refrigerator for up to 3 days.

BAKING TIP: The dough will be slightly thicker than cake batter.

TROUBLESHOOTING TIP: Sourdough bread rises more slowly than traditional yeast breads. Allow an additional hour or two if needed to let your bread rise until it is about 1 inch below the top of the loaf pan.

cinnamon-raisin bread

PREP TIME: 10 minutes, plus 40 minutes to rise • **COOK TIME:** 55 minutes

Sweet raisins, sugar, and spicy cinnamon transform everyday sandwich bread into an extra-special treat. Because gluten-free bread dough is much looser than dough made with wheat flour, the add-ins are stirred in after the dough has been poured into the pan.

MAKES 1 LOAF

TOOLS

- 9-by-5-inch loaf pan
- Parchment paper
- Stand mixer (optional)

3 cups White Bread Flour Blend (page 10)

6 tablespoons granulated sugar, divided

1 tablespoon double-acting, aluminum-free, gluten-free baking powder

1 packet (2¼ teaspoons) active dry yeast

1½ teaspoons xanthan gum

1 teaspoon sea salt

2 teaspoons ground cinnamon, divided

1½ cups water, milk, or nondairy milk, warmed to 110°F

2 eggs, at room temperature

3 tablespoons canola oil

1½ teaspoons apple cider vinegar

½ cup raisins

2 tablespoons brown sugar

1. Preheat the oven to 300°F for about 1 minute, until it reaches a temperature of 80°F. Turn off the heat.

2. Line a loaf pan with parchment paper.

3. Place the flour blend, 4 tablespoons of sugar, baking powder, yeast, xanthan gum, salt, and ½ teaspoon of cinnamon into the bowl of a stand mixer or a large bowl. Mix just to combine the dry ingredients.

4. Add the water or milk, eggs, oil, and vinegar, and mix for 15 seconds. Scrape down the sides of the bowl with a spatula, and mix on medium speed for 3 minutes.

5. Pour half of the bread batter into the prepared pan (see Baking tip).

6. In a small bowl, mix the remaining 2 tablespoons of sugar, remaining 1½ teaspoons ground cinnamon, and raisins. Sprinkle half the mixture over the batter. Use a butter knife to swirl the mixture, using up-and-down and back-and-forth strokes.

7. Repeat with the remaining batter and remaining cinnamon-raisin mixture.

8. Place the pan in the oven and allow the batter to rise for 30 minutes. It should not crest the sides of the pan.

9. Remove the pan from the oven, then preheat the oven to 375°F while the batter continues to rise at room temperature for 10 more minutes.

CONTINUED ➤

cinnamon-raisin bread CONTINUED

10. Bake for 55 minutes. Remove the pan from the oven, and allow to rest for 2 minutes. Run a knife along the sides of the pan, and invert it onto a cooling rack. Allow the bread to cool on its side completely before slicing.

11. Serve or store in a tightly sealed zip-top bag in the refrigerator for up to 3 days.

BAKING TIP: The batter will be just a little thicker than cake batter.

TROUBLESHOOTING TIP: Avoid distributing the raisins and sugar all the way to the bottom or sides of the pan, where the direct heat can burn them.

pumpernickel bread

PREP TIME: 10 minutes, plus 40 minutes to rise • **COOK TIME:** 55 minutes

Although this round, sliceable bread is usually made with rye flour, which contains gluten, it is the ground caraway seeds, molasses, and cocoa that give this bread its pronounced flavor. Because the dough is much looser, the loaf cannot be baked free-form. I like using a round cake pan.

MAKES 1 LOAF

TOOLS

- 9-inch round cake pan
- Parchment paper
- Stand mixer (optional)

2 cups Multigrain Flour Blend (page 10)

¼ cup brown sugar

1 tablespoon cocoa powder

1 tablespoon caraway seeds

1 (¼-ounce) packet active dry yeast

2 teaspoons double-acting, aluminum-free, gluten-free baking powder

1 teaspoon xanthan gum

¾ teaspoon sea salt

1 teaspoon instant espresso powder (optional)

2 tablespoons canola oil

2 tablespoons molasses

1 cup water, milk, or non-dairy milk, warmed to 110°F

1 teaspoon apple cider vinegar

1. Preheat the oven to 300°F for about 1 minute, until it reaches 80°F. Turn off the heat.

2. Line the interior of a cake pan with parchment paper.

3. Place the flour blend, brown sugar, cocoa powder, caraway seeds, yeast, baking powder, xanthan gum, salt, and espresso powder (if using) into the bowl of a stand mixer or a large bowl. Mix just to combine the dry ingredients.

4. Add the oil, molasses, water, and vinegar to the bowl, and mix for 15 seconds. Scrape down the sides of the bowl with a spatula, and mix on medium speed for 3 minutes.

5. Pour the bread batter into the prepared pan. It will be slightly thicker than cake batter.

6. Place the pan in the oven and allow the batter to rise for 30 minutes. It should not crest the sides of the pan.

7. Remove the pan from the oven, then preheat the oven to 375°F while the batter continues to rise for 10 more minutes.

8. Bake for 55 minutes. Remove the pan from the oven, and allow to rest for 2 minutes. Run a knife along the sides of the pan, and invert it onto a cooling rack. Turn over and allow the bread to cool completely before slicing.

9. Serve or store in a tightly sealed zip-top bag in the refrigerator for up to 3 days.

INGREDIENT TIP: Dust the top of the loaf by sifting 1 tablespoon potato starch over the dough just before baking. This provides visual appeal for a crackled surface and also allows you to pat the bread with your hands to smooth it—without your hands sticking.

hearty nut and seed bread

PREP TIME: 10 minutes, plus 40 minutes to rise • **COOK TIME:** 55 minutes

This dense vegan loaf bread works fine for sandwiches—it's prepared in a traditional loaf pan—but it really shines as a base for avocado toast or simply toasted and slathered with butter.

MAKES 1 LOAF

TOOLS

- 9-by-5-inch loaf pan
- Parchment paper
- Stand mixer (optional)

2 cups Multigrain Flour Blend (page 10)

¼ cup ground flaxseed

3 tablespoons brown sugar

1 packet (2¼ teaspoons) active dry yeast

1½ teaspoons xanthan gum

1 teaspoon sea salt

3 tablespoons canola oil

1½ cups water, warmed to 110°F

½ cup gluten-free oats, plus 1 tablespoon

½ cup roughly chopped toasted hazelnuts

¼ cup sunflower seeds, plus 1 tablespoon

1. Preheat the oven to 300°F for about 1 minute, until it reaches 80°F. Turn off the heat.

2. Line the interior of a loaf pan with parchment paper.

3. Place the flour blend, flaxseed, brown sugar, yeast, xanthan gum, and salt into the bowl of a stand mixer or a large bowl. Mix just to combine the dry ingredients.

4. Add the oil and water, and mix for 15 seconds. Scrape down the sides of the bowl with a spatula, and mix on medium speed for 3 minutes.

5. Fold in ½ cup of oats, the hazelnuts, and ¼ cup of sunflower seeds.

6. Scrape the batter into the prepared pan. It will be slightly thicker than cake batter. Sprinkle with the remaining 1 tablespoon of oats and remaining 1 tablespoon of sunflower seeds.

7. Place the pan in the oven and allow the batter to rise for 30 minutes. It should not crest the sides of the pan.

8. Remove the pan from the oven, then preheat the oven to 375°F while the batter continues to rise for 10 more minutes.

9. Bake for 55 minutes. Remove the pan from the oven, and allow to rest for 2 minutes. Run a knife along the sides of the pan, and invert it onto a cooling rack. Allow the bread to cool on its side completely before slicing.

10. Serve or store in a tightly sealed zip-top bag in the refrigerator for up to 3 days.

INGREDIENT TIP: If you prefer not to use hazelnuts, you can make this with pecans, walnuts, or almonds.

potato bread

PREP TIME: 20 minutes, plus 8 hours to chill and 2 hours to rise • **COOK TIME:** 55 minutes

In this recipe, I veer away from fluffy potato breads and opt for a slightly heavier bread with a texture similar to pound cake and a subtle potato flavor.

MAKES 1 LOAF

TOOLS

- Medium pot
- Potato ricer (optional)
- Stand mixer (optional)
- Plastic wrap
- 9-by-5-inch loaf pan
- Parchment paper

For the potato

4 cups water

1 medium russet potato, peeled and diced

For the bread

3 cups Multigrain Flour Blend (page 10)

¼ cup sugar

1 packet (2¼ teaspoons) instant yeast

1 tablespoon double-acting, aluminum-free, gluten-free baking powder

1½ teaspoons xanthan gum

1¼ teaspoons sea salt

Potato and cooking liquid

4 tablespoons butter or nondairy butter, at room temperature

2 eggs, at room temperature

1½ teaspoons apple cider vinegar

1 tablespoon potato starch

To make the potato

1. In a medium pot over medium-high heat, heat the water and potato. Cover and cook for 12 minutes, until the potato is very tender. Drain, reserving ¾ cup of the cooking liquid.

2. Press the potatoes through a potato ricer into a medium bowl, or use a fork to mash them until no lumps remain. The yield should be roughly ¾ cup. Set aside.

To make the bread

1. Place the flour blend, sugar, yeast, baking powder, xanthan gum, and salt into the bowl of a stand mixer or large bowl. Mix just to combine the dry ingredients.

2. Add the potato, potato cooking liquid, butter, eggs, and vinegar, and mix for 15 seconds. Scrape down the sides of the bowl with a spatula, and mix on medium speed for 3 minutes.

3. Cover the bowl tightly with plastic wrap, and refrigerate for at least 8 hours but not more than 24 hours. Line a loaf pan with parchment paper.

4. Remove the dough from the refrigerator and scrape it into the prepared pan. Allow to rise for 2 hours, or until it nearly reaches the top of the pan.

5. Preheat the oven to 375°F.

6. Bake for 55 minutes. Remove from the oven, dust with the potato starch, and allow to rest for 2 minutes. Run a knife along the sides of the pan, and transfer the bread to a cooling rack. Allow the bread to cool on its side completely before slicing.

7. Serve or store in a tightly sealed zip-top bag in the refrigerator for up to 3 days.

INGREDIENT TIP: Make sure the potatoes and potato cooking liquid have cooled enough to touch comfortably with the inside of your wrist. This will ensure they're not so hot as to kill the yeast.

chapter six
Artisan Breads

multigrain baguette

PREP TIME: 15 minutes, plus 40 minutes to rise • **COOK TIME:** 35 minutes

This multigrain baguette has a more complex flavor and heartier texture than the French Baguette (page 22). This one is perfect for sopping up a flavorful chickpea purée or serving alongside a vegetarian soup.

MAKES 2 LOAVES

TOOLS

- French bread pan, perforated is okay
- Parchment paper
- Baking dish

2 cups Multigrain Flour Blend (page 10)

1 tablespoon sugar

1 packet (2¼ teaspoons) active dry yeast

1 teaspoon xanthan gum

1 teaspoon sea salt

1 cup water, warmed to 110°F

2 tablespoons canola oil, divided

1. Preheat the oven to 300°F for 1 minute, until it reaches a temperature of 80°F. Turn off the oven.

2. Line a French bread pan with parchment paper.

3. Sift the flour blend, sugar, yeast, xanthan gum, and salt into a medium bowl.

4. Add the water and 1 tablespoon of oil to the bowl, and mix for 30 seconds. Scrape down the sides of the bowl, and mix for 3 minutes.

5. Spoon the batter into the prepared pan to form 2 baguettes about 12 inches long. Gently smooth the top of the batter with a clean spatula, without flattening it, then brush the bread with the remaining 1 tablespoon of oil.

6. Place the pan in the oven and let the batter rise for 40 minutes, until it has nearly doubled in size. Remove from the oven.

7. Preheat the oven to 400°F. Place a baking dish filled with at least 2 cups of hot water on the bottom rack of the oven.

8. Place the pan on the center rack and bake for 35 minutes. The bread should have a hollow sound when tapped. Remove from the oven, and cool completely before slicing.

9. Serve or store in a tightly sealed zip-top bag in the refrigerator.

VARIATION TIP: Top this multigrain bread with 2 tablespoons each of gluten-free oats and poppy seeds before baking.

Adding Herbs or Seeds

You can add about ½ cup of herbs, nuts, seeds, fruit, or olives to gluten-free breads without compromising the structure of the bread. Try these suggested additions:

Seeds: After proofing but before baking, top yeast bread or quick breads with a handful of hulled sunflower seeds, sesame seeds, or pumpkin seeds.

Nuts: Fold roughly chopped and toasted pecans, walnuts, or hazelnuts into quick breads or yeast breads before proofing, or sprinkle a handful on top of quick breads or yeast breads before baking.

Fruit: Fold dried fruit, such as raisins, cranberries, cherries, or apricot pieces, into yeast breads before proofing or quick breads before baking.

Herbs: Fold 2 tablespoons minced fresh herbs or 1 tablespoon dried herbs into yeast breads before proofing. Alternately, make a paste of ¼ to ½ cup minced fresh herbs and 2 to 4 tablespoons olive oil, and spread the paste over yeast breads just before baking.

Olives: After all other ingredients are mixed, fold in pitted Kalamata olives and a tablespoon of rosemary to a traditional rustic round loaf.

boule

PREP TIME: 15 minutes, plus 45 minutes to 1 hour to rise • **COOK TIME:** 35 minutes

Boule is more a shape of French bread than it is a type of bread. In traditional baking, boule is made round by creating surface tension on dough shaped into a ball. The surface tension helps the bread rise up instead of out. With gluten-free baking, use two small, round cake pans or springform pans to achieve this effect.

MAKES 2 LOAVES

TOOLS

- 2 (6-inch) round cake pans

4½ teaspoons canola oil, divided

3 teaspoons brown rice flour, divided

2 cups White Bread Flour Blend (page 10)

1 packet (2¼ teaspoons) active dry yeast

2 teaspoons sugar

¾ teaspoon xanthan gum

¾ teaspoon sea salt

¾ cup water, warmed to 110°F

1 teaspoon potato starch

1. Preheat the oven to 300°F for 1 minute, until it reaches a temperature of 80°F. Turn off the oven.

2. Coat the inside of each cake pan (see Baking tip) with 1 teaspoon of oil and 1½ teaspoons of brown rice flour.

3. Sift the flour blend, yeast, sugar, xanthan gum, and salt into a medium bowl.

4. Add the water and remaining 2½ teaspoons of oil, and mix for 30 seconds. Scrape down the sides of the bowl, and mix for 3 additional minutes.

5. Spoon the batter into the prepared pans, mounding them slightly in the center. Smooth the tops with a clean spatula.

6. Sift the potato starch over the dough, and pat gently with your hands to smooth.

7. Place the pan in the oven and let the dough rise for 45 minutes to 1 hour, until risen but not doubled in size. Remove from the oven.

8. Preheat the oven to 425°F.

9. Bake on the center rack for 15 minutes. Reduce the heat to 375°F, and bake for another 15 to 20 minutes. The bread should have a hollow sound when tapped. Remove from the oven and cool completely before slicing.

10. Serve or store in a tightly sealed zip-top bag in the refrigerator for up to 3 days.

BAKING TIP: If you don't have smaller cake pans, you can bake one boule in a 9-inch cake pan. Increase cooking time to a total of 1 hour (15 minutes at 425°F and 45 minutes at 375°F).

sourdough baguette

PREP TIME: 15 minutes, plus 8 to 12 hours to prepare the starter and 3 to 4 hours to rise
COOK TIME: 35 minutes

Sourdough bread gets its distinct sourness not from the yeast, but from the lactic acid bacteria found in the dough. If you're lucky enough to live in San Francisco, you have instant access to *Lactobacillus sanfranciscensis*, which gives San Francisco sourdough its distinct sourness.

MAKES 2 LOAVES

TOOLS

- French bread pan, perforated is okay
- Parchment paper
- Baking dish

For the starter

½ cup Sourdough Starter (page 30)

½ cup filtered water

½ cup brown rice flour

For the bread

2 cups White Bread Flour Blend (page 10)

1 tablespoon sugar

1 teaspoon xanthan gum

1 teaspoon sea salt

½ cup Sourdough Starter

1 cup water, warmed to 110°F

½ tablespoon canola oil

To prepare the starter

1. Eight to 12 hours before you plan to make the sourdough bread, place the jar filled with sourdough starter (prepared according to the master tutorial instructions found on page 30) on the counter and feed it with ¼ cup water and ¼ cup brown rice flour at 4- to 6-hour intervals. Stir and cover the jar with a coffee filter. Allow to sit at room temperature for 8 to 12 hours.

2. Remove ½ cup of prepared starter that is required for this recipe, and return the rest of the master sourdough starter to the refrigerator.

To make the bread

1. Line a French bread pan with parchment paper.

2. Sift the flour blend, sugar, xanthan gum, and salt into a medium mixing bowl. Set aside.

3. Add the starter, water, and oil to the bowl, and mix for 30 seconds. Scrape down the sides of the bowl, and mix for 3 additional minutes.

4. Spoon the batter into the prepared pan to form 2 baguettes about 12 inches long. Smooth the top of the batter with a clean spatula without flattening it, then pat the top of the dough with wet hands to smooth it out.

CONTINUED ➤

5. Let the batter rise at room temperature for 3 to 4 hours, until it has nearly doubled in size.

6. Preheat the oven to 400°F. Place a baking dish filled with at least 2 cups of hot water on the bottom rack of the oven.

7. Bake on the center rack for 35 minutes. The bread should have a hollow sound when tapped. Allow to cool completely before slicing.

8. Serve or store in a tightly sealed zip-top bag in the refrigerator for up to 3 days.

BAKING TIP: Because sourdough bread rises more slowly, cover the rising loaves with an extra-large plastic container to prevent dust from falling on it.

ciabatta

PREP TIME: 10 minutes, plus 8 to 12 hours to prepare the starter and 1 hour 30 minutes to rise
COOK TIME: 25 minutes

Authentic ciabatta has a rustic appearance but a surprisingly soft, chewy, and elegant texture. While it's not a flat bread, it doesn't rise as significantly as, say, a sandwich bread or French bread. It works well for slicing in half horizontally and making sandwiches, dunking into olive oil, or turning into hand-torn croutons. Like other gluten-free bread doughs, this dough is very loose and cannot be baked free-form. I use a 6-by-10-inch baking dish to yield one medium loaf.

MAKES 1 LOAF

TOOLS

- 6-by-10-inch baking dish
- Parchment paper
- Stand mixer (optional)
- Baking dish

For the starter

½ cup Sourdough Starter (page 30)

½ cup filtered water

½ cup brown rice flour

For the bread

½ teaspoon active dry yeast

½ cup water, warmed to 110°F

2 teaspoons sugar

1 cup White Bread Flour Blend (page 10)

½ cup millet flour

1 teaspoon xanthan gum

1 teaspoon sea salt

1 teaspoon olive oil

½ cup Sourdough Starter

1 tablespoon brown rice flour

To prepare the starter

1. Eight to 12 hours before you plan to make the ciabatta, place the jar filled with sourdough starter (prepared according to the master tutorial instructions on page 30) on the counter and feed it with ¼ cup water and ¼ cup brown rice flour at 4- to 6-hour intervals. Stir and cover the jar with a coffee filter. Allow to sit at room temperature for 8 to 12 hours.

2. Remove ½ cup of prepared starter that is required for this recipe, and return the rest of the master sourdough starter to the refrigerator.

To make the bread

1. Line the interior of a 6-by-10-inch baking dish with parchment paper.

2. Place the yeast, water, and sugar in the bowl of a stand mixer or a large bowl. Stir to mix. Set aside.

3. In a separate bowl, sift together the flour blend, millet flour, xanthan gum, and salt.

4. When the yeast mixture is frothy, add in the dry ingredients, oil, and sourdough starter. Mix for 15 seconds. Scrape down the sides of the bowl with a spatula. Mix for 3 additional minutes.

CONTINUED ➤

ciabatta CONTINUED

5. Transfer the dough to the prepared baking dish. Smooth the top with a spatula. Sprinkle the brown rice flour over the dough, then dimple the top of the dough with your fingertips.

6. Cover the baking dish loosely with a damp cloth, and place the dish in a warm place to let the dough rise for 1 hour and 30 minutes. It will not rise significantly during this time but will continue to rise once it is in the oven.

7. Preheat the oven to 425°F. Place a baking dish with 2 cups of hot water on the bottom rack of the oven.

8. Bake the ciabatta for 22 minutes. Transfer the loaf to a wire rack to cool.

9. Serve or store in a tightly sealed zip-top bag in the refrigerator for up to 3 days.

BAKING TIP: To apply the brown rice flour evenly over the top of the bread, use a wire mesh strainer to lightly dust the bread.

challah

PREP TIME: 10 minutes, plus 45 minutes to rise • **COOK TIME:** 30 minutes

Challah is a braided, enriched bread served on the Sabbath in Jewish communities—and everywhere it's served, people enjoy a tender, chewy, barely sweet egg bread. It makes an excellent addition to family brunch and can be used to create amazing French toast. Gluten-free dough is more difficult to braid than traditional wheat dough, but with a little patience, it can absolutely be done.

MAKES 1 LOAF

TOOLS

- Parchment paper
- Baking sheet

2¼ cups White Bread Flour Blend (page 10), plus more for dusting

2 tablespoons sugar

1 (¼-ounce) packet active dry yeast

1¼ teaspoons xanthan gum

¾ teaspoon sea salt

3 eggs, at room temperature, divided

½ cup milk or nondairy milk, warmed to 110°F

3 tablespoons butter or nondairy butter, at room temperature

1 tablespoon water

1. Sift the flour blend, sugar, yeast, xanthan gum, and salt into a mixing bowl.

2. Separate 1 egg over a small glass jar, reserving the white. Add the egg yolk to the flour blend mixture along with the remaining 2 eggs, milk, and butter. Mix for 30 seconds. Scrape down the sides of the bowl, and mix for 3 additional minutes.

3. Line a clean work surface with parchment paper. Sprinkle it generously with additional flour blend.

4. Divide the dough into 3 portions and gently roll each into a very soft 8-inch log shape.

5. Line up the dough pieces next to one another and pinch them all together at one end. Carefully braid the dough, using a classic three-strand braid. Brush away the excess flour and carefully slide the parchment paper containing the braid onto a baking sheet.

6. Allow the dough to rise for 45 minutes, until it has risen but not doubled in size. Remove from the oven.

7. Preheat the oven to 400°F.

8. Whisk the reserved egg white with the water, and very gently brush the mixture over the risen dough so as not to degas it (cause it to fall).

CONTINUED >

challah

9. Place the baking sheet on the center rack of the oven and reduce the heat to 350°F. Bake for 30 minutes. The bread should have a hollow sound when tapped. Remove from the oven, and cool completely before slicing.

10. Serve or store in a tightly sealed zip-top bag in the refrigerator for up to 3 days.

BAKING TIP: Traditional challah is made using four or more strands to braid. However, given the consistency of gluten-free dough, I opt for a three-strand braid. If you're feeling adventurous, find a tutorial online for shaping challah and give it a try! If you find braiding the dough too challenging, you can also place the dough in a nonstick braided bread mold loaf pan or silicone mold.

crostini

PREP TIME: 5 minutes • **COOK TIME:** 10 minutes

Crostini (small slices of toasted bread) make the perfect party appetizer and make good use of day-old French Baguette. The Multigrain Baguette (page 44) also works well in this recipe. These are quick to make but don't store very well, so for the best texture, make them just before you intend to serve them.

MAKES 24 CROSTINI

TOOLS

• Baking sheet

1 French Baguette (page 22)

4 tablespoons extra-virgin olive oil, divided

1. Preheat the oven to 400°F.

2. Cut the baguette into ½-inch-thick slices. Spread the slices in a single layer on a rimmed baking sheet. Brush the tops with 2 tablespoons of oil.

3. Bake for 5 to 7 minutes, until golden brown. Turn the slices over, brush with the remaining 2 tablespoons of oil, and bake for another 2 to 3 minutes, until just crisp.

4. Allow to cool completely before serving or storing in a covered container.

VARIATION TIP: To make curved crostini, press the slices of baguette into a muffin tin before brushing with 2 tablespoons olive oil, then bake for 5 to 7 minutes. These hold toppings quite handily!

garlic and herb croutons

PREP TIME: 5 minutes • **COOK TIME:** 10 minutes

These croutons are perfect for topping salads or making a delicious panzanella or bread salad. Change up the herbs as you see fit. I love using minced fresh tarragon, basil, parsley, and thyme.

MAKES 4 CUPS

TOOLS

- Baking sheet

¼ cup extra-virgin olive oil

1 teaspoon garlic powder

1 teaspoon herbes de Provence

½ teaspoon sea salt

1 French Baguette (page 22)

1. Preheat the oven to 325°F.

2. In a medium bowl, whisk the oil, garlic powder, herbes de Provence, and salt.

3. Cut the baguette into ½-inch slices, then cut these into ½-inch cubes. Place them in the bowl with the olive oil mixture, and toss gently to coat.

4. Spread the bread cubes in a single layer on a rimmed baking sheet.

5. Bake for 5 to 7 minutes, until golden brown.

6. Allow to cool completely before serving or storing in a covered container.

VARIATION TIP: To make plain croutons, omit the garlic and herbes de Provence.

bread crumbs

PREP TIME: 5 minutes • **COOK TIME:** 5 minutes

Bread crumbs work well as a binder in meatballs, crab cakes, and vegetarian burgers. They're a great way to use up leftover bread and can be made ahead of time and frozen for later use.

MAKES 2 CUPS

TOOLS

- Food processor
- Rimmed baking sheet

1 one-day-old French Baguette (page 22)

1. Preheat the oven to 325°F.

2. Tear the baguette into 1-inch pieces. Place them in a food processor, and pulse until they are ground into coarse crumbs.

3. Spread the crumbs on a rimmed baking sheet and bake for 2 to 3 minutes, until just dried out.

4. Allow to cool completely before serving or storing in a zip-top bag.

VARIATION TIP: Freeze the bread crumbs in ½-cup portions so you can use just what you need.

chapter seven
Rolls and Bagels

BISCUITS, PAGE 58

biscuits

PREP TIME: 10 minutes • **COOK TIME:** 15 minutes

These soft, tender biscuits are the perfect vehicle for a gamut of options: savory sausage gravy, sweet strawberries and cream, or nothing more than a pat of butter. The trick to making them light as a feather is not to overprocess when mixing the dough. You should still see small chunks of butter.

MAKES 8 BISCUITS

TOOLS

- Food processor
- Baking sheet

2 cups Multigrain Flour Blend (page 10)

1 tablespoon double-acting, aluminum-free, gluten-free baking powder

½ teaspoon sea salt

¼ teaspoon xanthan gum

6 tablespoons (¾ stick) cold butter or nondairy butter, cut into small pieces

½ cup milk or nondairy milk

Potato starch, for dusting

1. Preheat the oven to 450°F.

2. In a food processor, combine the flour blend, baking powder, salt, and xanthan gum, and pulse once or twice just to integrate.

3. Add the pieces of butter to the food processor, and pulse a few times.

4. Pour in the milk and blend just until integrated but tiny pieces of butter are still visible.

5. Dust a clean work surface with potato starch. Turn the dough out of the food processor and coat with the starch. Carefully roll the dough out to about 1½ inches thick.

6. Use a small glass to cut the dough into circles, or cut it into squares. Transfer to a baking sheet. Bake for 12 to 14 minutes, until puffy and golden brown.

INGREDIENT TIP: Use unsweetened almond milk, soy milk, or coconut milk as well as a dairy-free butter to make this recipe dairy-free.

multigrain pull-apart rolls

PREP TIME: 10 minutes, plus 45 minutes to rise • **COOK TIME:** 25 minutes

For a healthier dinner roll, try these savory buns. They have a slightly nuttier flavor than the Dinner Rolls (page 24) and are perfect served with rustic soups and stews. You can use either the Multigrain Flour Blend or the Oat Flour Blend (page 10).

MAKES 8 ROLLS

TOOLS

- 9-inch round cake pan
- Parchment paper

2 cups plus 1 tablespoon Multigrain Flour Blend (page 10), divided

1 tablespoon sugar

1 (¼-ounce) packet active dry yeast

1½ teaspoons xanthan gum

1 teaspoon sea salt

¾ cup water, warmed to 110°F

2 tablespoons butter, at room temperature, divided

2 eggs, at room temperature

1. Preheat the oven to 300°F for 1 minute, until it reaches a temperature of 80°F. Turn off the oven.

2. Line the interior of a 9-inch round cake pan with parchment paper. Set aside.

3. In a large bowl, mix together the flour blend, sugar, yeast, xanthan gum, and salt.

4. Add the water, 1 tablespoon of butter, and the eggs. Mix for 30 seconds. Scrape down the sides of the bowl with a spatula. Mix for 3 minutes.

5. Divide the mixture into 8 portions and place them into the cake pan.

6. Place the pan in the warmed oven and let the dough rise for 45 minutes.

7. Remove the pan from the oven. Preheat the oven to 375°F.

8. Melt the remaining 1 tablespoon of butter, and brush it on the tops of the buns. Bake for 25 minutes, until the tops are golden brown.

BAKING TIP: You can also make these rolls in a muffin tin. Simply reduce the baking time by about 2 minutes. For a classic presentation, drop them into the muffin tin in 3 spoonsful.

cranberry-oat-walnut buns

PREP TIME: 10 minutes, plus 30 minutes to rise • **COOK TIME:** 25 minutes

Oat Bakery is a small artisan bakery near my home in Santa Barbara and crafts these exquisite Scandinavian breads using oat flour as the primary ingredient. The breads are dense, chewy, and nutritious. I created this gluten-free version of Oat Bakery's cranberry-walnut buns to go with Christmas dinner, and they were the star of our holiday table. My husband, Rich, said that these were perhaps the best bread I had ever made—gluten-free or not—as he snuck the last bun out of the basket.

MAKES 6 BUNS

TOOLS

- Hamburger bun pan or 6 ceramic ramekins

2 cups Oat Flour Blend (page 10)

¼ cup ground flaxseed

1 tablespoon minced rosemary

1 tablespoon brown sugar

1 (¼-ounce) packet active dry yeast

1½ teaspoons xanthan gum

1 teaspoon sea salt

1 cup water, warmed to 110°F

2 tablespoons extra-virgin olive oil, divided

½ cup roughly chopped toasted walnuts

½ cup dried cranberries

1. Preheat the oven to 300°F for 1 minute, until it reaches a temperature of 80°F. Turn off the oven.

2. In a large bowl, mix together the flour blend, flaxseed, rosemary, brown sugar, yeast, xanthan gum, and salt.

3. Add the water and 1 tablespoon of oil. Mix for 30 seconds. Scrape down the sides of the bowl with a spatula. Mix for 3 minutes.

4. Fold in the walnuts and dried cranberries.

5. Divide the mixture between the spaces in a hamburger bun pan (see Baking tip), mounding the dough in the center of each bun.

6. Place the pan in the warmed oven and let the dough rise for 30 minutes. Remove the pan from the oven.

7. Preheat the oven to 375°F.

8. Brush the tops of the buns with the remaining 1 tablespoon of oil. Bake for 25 minutes, until the tops of the buns are golden brown.

BAKING TIP: If you don't have a hamburger bun pan, you can use 6 ceramic ramekins coated with oil and dusted with gluten-free flour.

VARIATION TIP: Use whatever combination of herbs and nuts suits your taste. Try pumpkin seeds and minced dried apricot.

savory pesto rolls

PREP TIME: 10 minutes, plus 45 minutes to rise • **COOK TIME:** 25 minutes

Step aside, plain dinner rolls. These flavorful rolls have delicious basil and garlic pesto swirled into them that will make them the new star of your table. They're delicious as an accompaniment to Italian food or as the bread for deli sandwiches.

MAKES 8 ROLLS

TOOLS

- 8-inch round cake pan
- Parchment paper

2 cups White Bread Flour Blend (page 10)

1 tablespoon sugar

1 (¼-ounce) packet active dry yeast

1½ teaspoons xanthan gum

1 teaspoon sea salt

¾ cup water, heated to 110°F

2 eggs, at room temperature

3 tablespoons extra-virgin olive oil, divided

½ cup store-bought pesto

1. Preheat the oven to 300°F for 1 minute, until it reaches a temperature of 80°F. Turn off the oven.

2. Line the interior of an 8-inch round cake pan with parchment paper. Set aside.

3. In a large bowl, mix together the flour blend, sugar, yeast, xanthan gum, and salt.

4. Add the water, eggs, and 2 tablespoons of oil. Whisk for 30 seconds, then scrape down the sides of the bowl. Mix for 3 minutes.

5. Fold in the pesto, but do not fully mix, so swirls remain.

6. Divide the mixture into 8 portions and place them into the cake pan. Place the pan in the warmed oven and let the dough rise for 45 minutes.

7. Remove the pan from the oven. Preheat the oven to 375°F.

8. Brush the tops of the rolls with the remaining 1 tablespoon of oil. Bake for 25 minutes, until the tops are golden brown.

INGREDIENT TIP: There are dairy-free and nut-free pestos if you need to avoid those ingredients. Alternately, you can easily make your own by combining 1 cup roughly chopped fresh basil with 1 garlic clove, ¼ teaspoon lemon zest, ¼ teaspoon sea salt, and ¼ cup extra-virgin olive oil. Blend in a food processor until smooth.

hawaiian rolls

PREP TIME: 10 minutes, plus 15 minutes to prepare the sponge and 45 minutes to rise
COOK TIME: 25 minutes

Sweet, fragrant Hawaiian rolls are equally at home at holiday brunches or for serving tangy pulled pork at backyard barbecues. The potato starch in the flour blend keeps them nice and light, while the sweet rice flour gives them a satisfying chewy quality.

MAKES 12 ROLLS

TOOLS

- 8-by-10-inch baking dish
- Parchment paper

4 tablespoons water, divided

1 tablespoon instant yeast

3¼ cups plus 2 tablespoons White Bread Flour Blend (page 10), divided

⅓ cup brown sugar

2 teaspoons xanthan gum

1¼ teaspoons sea salt

½ cup canned pineapple juice

4 tablespoons butter, at room temperature, divided

2 large eggs plus 1 egg yolk, white reserved

1 teaspoon vanilla extract

1. Preheat the oven to 300°F for 1 minute, until it reaches a temperature of 80°F. Turn off the oven.

2. Line the interior of an 8-by-10-inch baking dish with parchment paper. Set aside.

3. Whisk together 2 tablespoons of water, the yeast, and ¼ cup of the flour blend in a small glass measuring cup to make a sponge. Set aside for about 15 minutes.

4. In a large mixing bowl, mix together the remaining 3 cups plus 2 tablespoons of the flour blend, brown sugar, xanthan gum, and salt.

5. Add the sponge, pineapple juice, butter, eggs plus egg yolk, and vanilla. Mix for 30 seconds. Scrape down the sides of the bowl with a spatula. Mix for 3 minutes.

6. Drop the dough by large spoonsful into the baking dish, not quite touching each other. Smooth the tops with wet hands, without flattening.

7. Place the baking dish in the warmed oven and let the dough rise for 45 minutes.

8. Remove the baking dish from the oven, then preheat the oven to 375°F.

9. Whisk the reserved egg white with the remaining 2 tablespoons of water, and brush over the rolls just before baking.

10. Bake for 22 to 25 minutes, until the tops are golden brown.

INGREDIENT TIP: This recipe calls for instant yeast and begins the dough with a sponge, both of which are helpful when working with a sweet and acidic dough like this one. Creating a sponge allows the yeast, flour, and water to interact and ferment, which enhances the flavor of the finished bread.

grain-free breadsticks

PREP TIME: 10 minutes, plus 20 minutes to rise • **COOK TIME:** 15 minutes

These breadsticks use my grain-free dough, because it is slightly stiffer than the other gluten-free doughs and prevents the breadsticks from spreading out all over the pan.

MAKES 8 BREADSTICKS

TOOLS

- Baking sheet
- Parchment paper

1 (¼-ounce) packet active dry yeast

1½ teaspoons sugar

⅓ cup water, heated to about 110°F

1 cup finely ground almond flour

¾ cup tapioca flour or tapioca starch

¼ cup potato starch

¾ teaspoon sea salt

1 egg white, whisked

1½ teaspoons red wine vinegar

2 tablespoons extra-virgin olive oil, divided

1. Preheat the oven to 300°F for 1 minute, until it reaches a temperature of 80°F. Turn off the oven.

2. In a small bowl, whisk together the yeast, sugar, and water. Set aside for 10 minutes.

3. In a medium bowl, mix together the almond flour, tapioca flour, potato starch, and salt.

4. Add the yeast mixture, egg white, and vinegar, and 1 tablespoon of oil to the almond flour mixture, and mix until just integrated.

5. Divide the mixture into 8 portions. Roll each into a 6-inch log, and place on a baking sheet lined with parchment paper. Brush the tops with the remaining 1 tablespoon of oil.

6. Set in the warmed oven to rise for 20 minutes.

7. Remove from the oven, then preheat the oven to 425°F.

8. Bake for 10 to 12 minutes, until just golden brown. Serve warm.

VARIATION TIP: For even more flavor, use a wire mesh strainer to sift 2 teaspoons garlic salt over the tops of the breadsticks before baking.

hamburger or hot dog buns

PREP TIME: 10 minutes, plus 20 minutes to rise • **COOK TIME:** 20 minutes

These hamburger buns have changed the game for our family grilling nights. Gone are the crumbly, stiff, commercially prepared gluten-free buns. These are soft and flexible, and stand up to burger patties without falling apart. After slicing, place the buns cut-side down on the grill to toast them gently.

MAKES 6 BUNS

TOOLS

- Hamburger or hot dog bun pan

2 cups White Bread Flour Blend (page 10)

1 tablespoon sugar

1 (¼-ounce) packet active dry yeast

1½ teaspoons xanthan gum

1 teaspoon sea salt

¾ cup water, heated to 110°F

2 eggs, at room temperature

1 tablespoon canola oil

2 tablespoons potato starch

1. Preheat the oven to 300°F for 1 minute, until it reaches a temperature of 80°F. Turn off the oven.

2. In a large bowl, mix together the flour blend, sugar, yeast, xanthan gum, and salt.

3. Add the water, eggs, and oil, and mix for 30 seconds. Scrape down the sides of the bowl with a spatula. Mix for 3 minutes.

4. Divide the mixture between the portions of the hamburger or hot dog bun pan. Smooth the tops with a spatula.

5. Sift the potato starch evenly over the buns, then pat them with clean hands so they're uniformly smooth.

6. Place the pan in the warmed oven and let the dough rise for 20 minutes.

7. Remove the pan from the oven, then preheat the oven to 375°F.

8. Bake for 20 minutes, or until the tops are golden brown. Allow to cool completely before slicing in half.

VARIATION TIP: To make a vegan version of these buns, use ⅓ cup aquafaba, which is the brine from canned chickpeas, in place of the eggs.

bagels

PREP TIME: 10 minutes, plus 20 minutes to rise • **COOK TIME:** 35 minutes

Admittedly, gluten-free bagels were the most intimidating recipe to develop. But in testing them, what a surprise! Boiling bagels is not much different than boiling ravioli—there's no need to be scared! Unlike other doughs in this book, the gluten-free dough can really be handled and more closely resembles typical bread dough.

MAKES 8 BAGELS

TOOLS

- Rimmed baking sheet
- Parchment paper
- Large pot

3½ cups White Bread Flour Blend (page 10), plus more for dusting

2 tablespoons sugar

1 (¼-ounce) packet active dry yeast

2 teaspoons xanthan gum

1 teaspoon sea salt

1 cup water, warmed to 110°F

2 tablespoons canola oil

1 egg, at room temperature, plus 1 egg white

8 cups water, plus 1 tablespoon

1 tablespoon molasses or brown sugar

1. Preheat the oven to 300°F for 1 minute, until it reaches a temperature of 80°F. Turn off the oven.

2. In a large bowl, mix together the flour blend, sugar, yeast, xanthan gum, and salt.

3. Add the water, oil, and egg, and stir for 30 seconds. Scrape down the sides of the bowl with a spatula. Mix for 3 minutes.

4. Sprinkle a clean work surface with a handful of the flour blend. Place the dough onto the floured surface and turn over a few times to coat. Divide the mixture into 4 pieces and then cut each of these in half.

5. Form each piece into a flattened disc and then poke your finger through to make a hole in the center. Stretch the hole slightly between two fingers. When the dough rises, it will make the hole smaller.

6. Place the shaped bagels on a rimmed baking sheet lined with parchment paper. Place them in the warmed oven to rise for 20 minutes.

7. Meanwhile, in a large pot, bring 8 cups of water and the molasses to a gentle boil. After the bagels have risen, place 2 or 3 at a time into the water, and cook for 2 minutes on each side. Using a slotted spoon or a spider, transfer them to a rack to drain. Repeat with the remaining bagels.

8. Preheat the oven to 425°F. Return the boiled bagels to the lined baking sheet.

9. Whisk the egg white with the remaining 1 tablespoon of water, and brush over the bagels.

10. Bake for 10 minutes. Reduce the heat to 400°F, and bake for another 15 minutes. Allow the bagels to cool completely before slicing and serving.

bialys

PREP TIME: 10 minutes, plus 1 hour to prepare the sponge and 20 minutes to rise
COOK TIME: 15 minutes

Bialys are chewy yeast rolls that originated in Poland and became popular in New York City. They're similar to bagels but are baked, not boiled. Also, instead of a hole in the center, bialys have a sunken center filled with a savory onion and poppy seed filling. For added flavor, I make this version with a sponge (see Ingredient tip).

MAKES 8 BIALYS

TOOLS

- Rimmed baking sheet
- Parchment paper

For the onion topping

½ cup minced onion

1 tablespoon canola oil

2 teaspoons poppy seeds

½ teaspoon sea salt

For the bialys

3½ cups White Bread Flour Blend (page 10), divided, plus more for dusting

1 (¼-ounce) packet active dry yeast

1 cup water, warmed to 110°F

1 tablespoon sugar

2 teaspoons xanthan gum

1 teaspoon sea salt

1 egg, at room temperature

2 tablespoons canola oil

To make the onion topping

Combine the onion, oil, poppy seeds, and salt in a small bowl. Set aside.

To make the bialys

1. In a medium bowl, mix ½ cup of flour blend with the yeast and water to make a sponge. Cover and set aside for 1 hour.

2. In a large bowl, mix together the remaining 3 cups of flour blend, sugar, xanthan gum, and salt.

3. Add the sponge, egg, and oil to the large bowl, and stir for 30 seconds. Scrape down the sides of the bowl with a spatula. Mix for 3 minutes.

4. Sprinkle a clean work surface with a handful of the flour blend. Place the dough onto the floured surface and turn over a few times to coat. Divide the mixture into 4 pieces, and then cut each of these in half.

5. Form each piece into a flattened disc, and then use your fingers to press a slight depression in the center, leaving about 1 inch all around.

6. Place the shaped bialys on a rimmed baking sheet lined with parchment paper. Divide the onion topping among the bialys' indentations. Allow the bialys to rise for 20 minutes.

7. Preheat the oven to 425°F.

8. Bake for 12 minutes. Remove from the oven, and allow to cool for 15 minutes (see Baking tip).

BAKING TIP: In traditional baking, bialys are sometimes softened before serving. After they cool for 15 minutes, place them in a zip-top bag for 10 minutes before serving to soften slightly.

INGREDIENT TIP: Creating a sponge allows the yeast, flour, and water to interact and ferment, which enhances the flavor of the finished bread.

submarine sandwich rolls

PREP TIME: 15 minutes, plus 40 minutes to rise • **COOK TIME:** 30 minutes

These small loaves work nicely for sub sandwiches or miniature baguettes to pack with lunch. They're especially good toasted and used for making *banh mi*, a Vietnamese sandwich, or for making meatball subs.

MAKES 4 ROLLS

TOOLS

- French bread pan, perforated is okay
- Parchment paper

1½ cups White Bread Flour Blend (page 10)

2 tablespoons sugar

1 (¼-ounce) packet active dry yeast

1 teaspoon xanthan gum

1 teaspoon sea salt

¾ cup water, warmed to 110°F

½ tablespoon canola oil

1. Preheat the oven to 300°F for 1 minute, until it reaches a temperature of 80°F. Turn off the oven.

2. Line a French bread pan with parchment paper.

3. Into a medium bowl, sift the flour blend, sugar, yeast, xanthan gum, and salt.

4. Add the water and oil, and mix for 30 seconds. Scrape down the sides of the bowl, and mix for 3 additional minutes.

5. Spoon the batter into the prepared pan and shape the batter into 4 rolls, each about 6 inches long, and place in the prepared pan. Smooth the tops with a clean spatula, then use wet hands to gently pat the tops to smooth them out more.

6. Place the pan in the oven and let the batter rise for 40 minutes, until it has nearly doubled in size. Remove from the oven.

7. Preheat the oven to 425°F.

8. Bake the bread on the center rack for 15 minutes. Reduce the heat to 375°F, and continue to bake for another 15 minutes. The bread should have a hollow sound when tapped. Allow to cool completely before slicing.

9. Serve or store in a zip-top bag in the refrigerator for up to 3 days.

BAKING TIP: Smaller loaves require less baking time than traditional French bread. If you choose to shape the loaves into 6 rolls instead of 4, reduce baking time slightly.

crumpets

PREP TIME: 10 minutes, plus 30 minutes to ferment • **COOK TIME:** 20 minutes

Crumpets are similar to English muffins, but the batter is thinner—more like a pancake batter—and they utilize baking soda to create dozens of tiny holes in the dough for collecting melted butter. Delicious, right?

MAKES 10 CRUMPETS

TOOLS

- Griddle or large nonstick skillet
- 10 (3- to 4-inch) English muffin rings (see Baking tip)

1¾ cups White Bread Flour Blend (page 10)

1 tablespoon sugar

1 (¼-ounce) packet active dry yeast

1¼ teaspoons sea salt

1 teaspoon double-acting, aluminum-free, gluten-free baking powder

½ teaspoon xanthan gum

¾ cup water, warmed to 110°F

½ cup milk or nondairy milk, warmed to 110°F

2 tablespoons butter, melted, plus more for greasing

1. In a large bowl, mix together the flour blend, sugar, yeast, salt, baking powder, and xanthan gum.

2. Add the water, milk, and butter, and whisk for 30 seconds. Scrape down the sides of the bowl. Mix for another 2 minutes. Set the mixture aside for 30 minutes to ferment slightly.

3. Heat a griddle or a large nonstick skillet over medium-high heat.

4. Grease the interior of the English muffin rings with butter.

5. Place as many rings onto the griddle or skillet as will fit, and fill each ring with about ¼ cup of batter. Cook for 3 to 5 minutes, then use tongs to carefully lift the ring from each crumpet. Continue cooking for another 10 minutes. Flip the crumpets and cook for another 5 minutes. Transfer to a cooling rack.

6. Repeat with the remaining batter. Serve warm.

BAKING TIP: If you don't have English muffin rings, crumpets can also be made using a tuna can with the lid and bottom removed. However, the sharp edges might make it a little more difficult to manage.

chapter eight

Flatbreads and Pizza

focaccia

PREP TIME: 10 minutes, plus 30 minutes to rise • **COOK TIME:** 50 minutes

This focaccia is better than any of the focaccia breads I ate while I still ate wheat. This version is sweet, chewy, and perfectly hearty. It is exactly what I'm looking for as a complement to dinner, and I hope you'll agree.

MAKES 1 LOAF

TOOLS

- Rimmed baking sheet
- Parchment paper

2 cups Multigrain Flour Blend (page 10)

2 tablespoons sugar

1 (¼-ounce) packet active dry yeast

1 teaspoon xanthan gum

½ teaspoon sea salt

¾ cup water, warmed to 110°F

2 eggs

2 tablespoons canola oil

1. Preheat the oven to 300°F for 1 minute, until it reaches a temperature of 80°F. Turn off the oven.

2. Line a rimmed baking sheet with parchment paper.

3. Into a medium bowl, sift the flour blend, sugar, yeast, xanthan gum, and salt.

4. Add the water, eggs, and oil, and mix for 30 seconds. Scrape down the sides of the bowl, and mix for 3 minutes.

5. On the prepared baking sheet, shape the dough into a rectangle about 8 inches by 10 inches. Dimple the dough with your fingertips and allow to rise for 30 minutes until it has increased in size by about half.

6. Preheat the oven to 400°F.

7. Place the baking sheet on the center rack of the oven, and reduce the heat to 350°F. Bake for 50 minutes. The focaccia should have a hollow sound when tapped. Allow to cool completely before slicing.

8. Serve or store in a zip-top bag in the refrigerator for up to 3 days.

VARIATION TIP: You can add herbs to this bread by either folding them into the dough or sprinkling them on top before baking.

roasted garlic and parsley hearthbreads

PREP TIME: 15 minutes, plus 45 minutes to rise • **COOK TIME:** 1 hour 5 minutes, including roasting the garlic

One of my first cookbooks was Nigella Lawson's *How to Be a Domestic Goddess*. I cooked my way through it, schmearing the pages with chocolate and olive oil and dusting them with flour. When I went gluten-free seven years ago, I placed the book on the shelf with resignation. In doing so, I found that the recipe I missed the most was her garlic and parsley hearthbreads—thick flatbreads, laden with parsley and roasted garlic, and dripping with olive oil. But thankfully, it's back. And like the original, this gluten-free version is soft, chewy, and perfectly indulgent.

SERVES 6

TOOLS

- Aluminum foil
- Rimmed baking sheet
- Parchment paper
- Blender

1 head garlic

7 tablespoons plus 1 teaspoon extra-virgin olive oil, divided

1 cup finely ground almond flour

¾ cup tapioca flour or tapioca starch

¼ cup potato starch

1 (¼-ounce) packet active dry yeast

1½ teaspoons sugar

1 teaspoon sea salt, divided

⅓ cup water, heated to about 110°F

1 egg white, whisked

1½ teaspoons red wine vinegar

1 tablespoon cornmeal or brown rice flour

1 cup roughly chopped fresh parsley

1. To roast the garlic, preheat the oven to 400°F. Cut the top off the head of garlic. Place the garlic on a square of aluminum foil and drizzle with 1 teaspoon of oil. Wrap the garlic in the foil.

2. Place the wrapped garlic directly on the center oven rack. Roast for 45 minutes, until the garlic is golden brown and soft. Open the packet of foil and allow the garlic to cool completely before handling.

3. Meanwhile, in a medium bowl, mix the almond flour, tapioca flour, potato starch, yeast, sugar, and ¾ teaspoon of salt. Add the water, egg white, vinegar, and 1 tablespoon of oil. Mix until just blended.

4. Line a rimmed baking sheet with parchment paper, and sprinkle with the cornmeal. Spread the dough onto the prepared surface, and smooth it out into a rectangle about 8 inches by 10 inches. Dimple the surface of the bread with your fingertips several times. Allow the dough to rise in a warm place for about 45 minutes, until doubled in size.

CONTINUED ▶

5. When the garlic is cool enough to handle, squeeze the cloves out and place them into a blender along with the parsley, the remaining 6 tablespoons of oil, and the remaining ¼ teaspoon of salt. Purée until brilliant green but still slightly chunky, scraping down the sides of the blender with a spatula as needed.

6. Drizzle the garlic-parsley mixture over the bread. Bake for 20 minutes, or until just golden brown and cooked through. Allow to rest for 10 minutes before slicing and serving.

INGREDIENT TIP: To save time, you can roast the garlic up to 3 days ahead of time, even any time you are using the oven for another task.

cauliflower pizza crust

PREP TIME: 10 minutes • **COOK TIME:** 25 minutes

I hesitated to include this nontraditional pizza crust in this book. But gluten-free cooking sometimes relies too heavily on processed starches, so it's nice to skip all of that for a more wholesome pizza crust. Top it with your favorite pizza toppings.

MAKES 1 (16-INCH) CRUST

TOOLS

- Food processor
- Baking dish
- Nut milk bag (optional)
- Pizza pan
- Parchment paper

1 large head cauliflower

½ cup grated Parmesan cheese

3 garlic cloves, minced

2 tablespoons coconut flour

1 tablespoon extra-virgin olive oil

1 tablespoon Italian herb blend

1 egg

½ teaspoon sea salt

Freshly ground black pepper

1. Preheat the oven to 400°F.

2. Using a food processor with a grater attachment, grate the cauliflower (see Ingredient tip). Place the grated cauliflower into a baking dish and microwave on high for 2 minutes. Stir and microwave again for 2 minutes. Set aside to cool.

3. When the cauliflower is cool enough to handle, place it into a nut milk bag or a clean kitchen towel, and wring out all of the excess moisture (see Troubleshooting tip).

4. Meanwhile, whisk together the Parmesan cheese, garlic, coconut flour, oil, herb blend, egg, and salt. Season with pepper.

5. Stir the cauliflower into the cheese mixture until thoroughly blended.

6. Line a pizza pan with parchment paper. Spread the cauliflower mixture onto the prepared pan, and press it firmly to form a thin crust.

7. Bake for 15 minutes, or until gently browned.

8. Top with your favorite toppings and bake for another 10 minutes.

INGREDIENT TIP: You can also grate the cauliflower manually. Just be careful of your fingers!

TROUBLESHOOTING TIP: To prevent the crust from being too soggy, be sure to wring all the moisture from the cauliflower before mixing the crust. If it's still a bit soggy, add another 5 minutes to the baking time.

grain-free pizza crust

PREP TIME: 15 minutes, plus 30 minutes to rise • **COOK TIME:** 20 minutes

For several years I avoided grains altogether, but I still craved a tender, chewy, crispy pizza crust. Finally, I developed this recipe for weekly family pizza nights. It is similar to the Roasted Garlic and Parsley Hearthbreads (page 73), but it's made without eggs. You can shape it as thick or as thin as you like—the thinner you roll the dough, the more crackerlike the crust will be. Unlike most gluten-free doughs, this one is thick, like traditional wheat-based doughs.

MAKES 2 (12-INCH) CRUSTS

TOOLS

- Parchment paper
- 2 pizza pans
- 2 pizza stones (optional)

½ cup plus 1 tablespoon warm water, heated to about 110°F

1 (¼-ounce) packet active dry yeast

1 tablespoon sugar

1¼ cups finely ground almond flour

1 cup tapioca starch

½ cup potato starch

1 teaspoon sea salt

1 tablespoon red wine vinegar

1 tablespoon extra-virgin olive oil, plus 1 teaspoon for shaping the dough (optional)

1. Preheat the oven to 300°F for 1 minute, until it reaches a temperature of 80°F. Turn off the oven.

2. Cut 2 large squares of parchment paper, and line 2 pizza pans.

3. In a small bowl, mix the warm water, yeast, and sugar. Set aside.

4. In a large bowl, mix the almond flour, tapioca starch, potato starch, and salt. Add the yeast mixture, vinegar, and 1 tablespoon of oil. Mix until just blended.

5. Divide the dough in half, and place each half onto a prepared pan. Use a spatula to smooth the dough into a large circle, or drizzle the 1 teaspoon of oil (if using) onto clean hands and use them to press the dough into a large circle.

6. Place the pans in the oven, and allow the dough to rise for 30 minutes.

7. Remove the pans from the oven, then preheat the oven to 400°F. If using pizza stones place them on the center rack while the oven is preheating.

8. Place the pizza pans in the oven, or slide the pizza dough and parchment from the pans onto the preheated pizza stones. Bake for 7 to 10 minutes (shorter for a thinner crust).

9. Top with whatever toppings you like, and bake for another 10 minutes.

BAKING TIP: To get a very thin crust, shape the dough into a flattened disc, top with a second sheet of parchment, and roll out using a rolling pin.

pita bread

PREP TIME: 10 minutes, plus 30 minutes to prepare the sponge and 20 minutes to rest
COOK TIME: 10 minutes

Pita breads are round flatbreads cut in half and then filled with whatever delicious things you wish to add to them. I like to fill them with hummus, a few fresh tomatoes, herbs, and olive oil. The dough is not unlike other bread doughs in this book. The key to getting these breads to puff properly is placing them in a very hot oven onto a preheated pizza stone. Even through the parchment, the stone will hit them with a blast of heat and give you that gorgeous risen bread with the welcoming hollow interior.

MAKES 8 PITAS

TOOLS

- Pizza stone
- Parchment paper
- Pizza peel or rimless baking sheet

1 cup water, warmed to 110°F

2¾ cups White Bread Flour Blend (page 10), divided

1 (¼-ounce) packet active dry yeast

1 teaspoon sugar

1 teaspoon sea salt

½ teaspoon xanthan gum

2 tablespoons extra-virgin olive oil

1. Mix the water with ½ cup of flour blend, yeast, and sugar to form a sponge. Set aside for 30 minutes.

2. Preheat the oven to 475°F. Place a pizza stone into the oven while it preheats.

3. In a large bowl, add the remaining 2¼ cups of the flour blend, salt, xanthan gum, oil, and the sponge. Mix for 15 seconds. Scrape down the sides of the bowl with a spatula. Mix for 3 minutes.

4. Cut 8 squares of parchment paper (see Baking tip). Divide the dough into 8 equal portions, and spread each piece out into a circle that reaches near the edge of the parchment.

5. Set the dough aside to rest for 20 minutes.

6. Use a pizza peel or a rimless baking sheet to slide 2 pieces of dough onto the preheated pizza stone. Bake for 4 to 6 minutes, until the bread is very puffy. Remove from the oven, and repeat with the remaining dough.

BAKING TIP: To prepare the parchment paper, remove 2 large squares and cut each into 4 smaller squares about 6 inches wide. You can also use an unheated baking sheet to bake the dough, but it will not puff up as significantly.

rosemary-almond crackers

PREP TIME: 5 minutes • **COOK TIME:** 15 minutes

These crackers are completely grain-free—making them a healthier option than some gluten-free breads and crackers—and they're a cinch to mix together and roll out. The one trick is to avoid burning them. They go from underdone to deeply browned in a matter of minutes. Don't let that dissuade you, though. Just set a timer and stand by.

MAKES 24 CRACKERS

TOOLS

- Parchment paper
- Rimmed baking sheet

2 cups almond flour

1 tablespoon minced fresh rosemary

2 teaspoons sugar

¾ teaspoon sea salt

1 tablespoon extra-virgin olive oil

1 to 2 tablespoons ice-cold water

1. Preheat the oven to 325°F.

2. In a bowl, stir together the almond flour, rosemary, sugar, and salt.

3. Add the oil and 1 tablespoon of cold water. Stir to blend, adding more water as needed until the mixture comes together into a ball.

4. Place the dough onto a sheet of parchment paper and shape into a rectangle. Top with another sheet of parchment, and roll thinly with a rolling pin. Transfer to a rimmed baking sheet, and cut the dough into 24 squares.

5. Bake for 10 to 12 minutes.

6. Cool completely before serving or storing in an airtight container for up to 3 days.

BAKING TIP: To help the crackers cook evenly, you can separate them on the baking sheet slightly before baking.

chickpea crackers

PREP TIME: 5 minutes • **COOK TIME:** 5 minutes

To fill the void in the gluten-free cracker arena, you'll want to try creative options like this one. These chickpea crackers are begging for some cool tzatziki or even, for extra chickpea goodness, some hummus.

MAKES 4 VERY LARGE CRACKERS (SERVES 8)

TOOLS

- Parchment paper
- Baking sheet

2 cups garbanzo bean flour

1 teaspoon double-acting, aluminum-free, gluten-free baking powder

1 teaspoon sea salt

⅓ cup water

2 tablespoons canola oil

1. Preheat the oven to 350°F.

2. In a bowl, mix together the garbanzo bean flour, baking powder, and salt. Drizzle in the water and oil, and stir until the mixture comes together into a ball.

3. Divide the dough into 4 pieces and place them, not touching, on a large piece of parchment paper.

4. One at a time, top a piece of dough with a second sheet of parchment paper, and roll the dough out until very thin. Remove the top piece of parchment, repeat with the remaining dough, then carefully slide the bottom parchment paper onto a baking sheet.

5. Bake for 5 minutes, or until the crackers are barely browned. Allow to cool before breaking apart and serving or storing in a covered container.

VARIATION TIP: Top these crackers with rosemary and flaky sea salt, or with toasted cumin and caraway seeds.

grain-free tortillas

PREP TIME: 5 minutes • **COOK TIME:** 50 minutes

I have experimented with so many different approaches to making tortillas, and I quickly tired of rolling out balls of dough, having them tear apart, making a huge mess, and breaking down in frustration. All my gluten-free baking friends know, as you probably do, too—the struggle is real! I finally settled on this grain-free version, which, instead of being rolled out, gets—wait for it—poured. While it isn't as "floury" as commercial tortillas, the texture is soft and the tortillas are pliable. As a bonus, it doesn't get as soggy when baked in enchiladas as grain-based tortillas do.

MAKES 16 TORTILLAS

TOOLS

- Blender
- Nonstick skillet

2 cups almond flour

1 cup arrowroot

1½ teaspoons sea salt

1½ cups warm water

Canola oil

1. In a blender, combine the almond flour, arrowroot, salt, and warm water. Pulse a few times, scraping down the sides as needed. Blend until smooth.

2. Heat a nonstick skillet over medium heat, and brush lightly with oil.

3. Pour about ¼ cup of batter into the pan, and tilt to coat the pan. Cook for about 2 minutes, then flip and cook for another minute. Transfer the cooked tortilla to a warm plate and cover with a clean cloth.

4. Repeat with the remaining batter, adding more oil to the pan as needed.

INGREDIENT TIP: Cornstarch is an acceptable substitute for arrowroot.

TROUBLESHOOTING TIP: You can also use a spatula to smooth the batter into the pan.

naan

PREP TIME: 10 minutes, plus 30 minutes to rest • **COOK TIME:** 15 minutes

This flatbread is an essential element to any good Indian meal. The technique for cooking the bread is a little bit intimidating, but it produces the best golden-brown exterior and a soft, chewy texture.

MAKES 6 FLATBREADS

TOOLS

- Stand mixer (optional)
- Plastic wrap
- Pizza stone or rimmed baking sheet (see Baking tip)

2½ cups White Bread Flour Blend (page 10)

1 tablespoon sugar

1 (¼-ounce) packet active dry yeast

1 teaspoon sea salt

½ teaspoon double-acting, aluminum-free, gluten-free baking powder

½ teaspoon xanthan gum

3 tablespoons milk or nondairy milk

1 egg, whisked

Oil, for greasing

2 tablespoons ghee or melted butter

1. Combine the flour blend, sugar, yeast, salt, baking powder, and xanthan gum in the bowl of a stand mixer fitted with the paddle attachment, or in a large bowl. Add the milk and egg. Mix for 15 seconds. Scrape down the sides of the bowl. Mix again for 3 minutes.

2. Grease a clean bowl with oil, and transfer the dough into it. Cover with plastic wrap and set aside for 30 minutes.

3. Preheat the oven to 450°F. Place a pizza stone on the bottom rack of the oven.

4. When the oven is hot, switch the heating method to broil.

5. Divide the dough into 6 pieces. Shape each into a circle about 4 inches wide.

6. Carefully place 2 or 3 of the dough circles onto the stone. Cook for 2 to 4 minutes, or until the naan is hot and gently browned. Brush the cooked bread with ghee and place in a basket, covering with a clean cloth. Repeat with the remaining dough.

BAKING TIP: Pizza stones can withstand the high heat of the broiler. If you need to use a rimmed baking sheet instead, do not preheat the pan. The breads will not brown as well and will take slightly longer to cook, but they'll still be delicious.

injera

PREP TIME: 10 minutes, plus 36 to 48 hours to ferment • **COOK TIME:** 30 minutes

Injera is an Ethiopian fermented flatbread made with teff flour, which is naturally gluten-free. Like all breads, injera has deep cultural roots dictating exactly how it should be prepared, including how long to ferment the batter, whether to use only teff flour, and whether to add yeast or chemical leaveners. I make no argument for the authenticity of the bread, but I can say for sure it is good for sopping up Ethiopian food!

MAKES 12 TO 16 FLATBREADS

TOOLS

- Plastic wrap
- 10- or 12-inch skillet

2 cups teff flour

¼ teaspoon active dry yeast

2 to 3 cups water, warmed to 110°F, divided

1 cup White Bread Flour Blend (page 10)

½ teaspoon sea salt

¼ teaspoon baking soda

1. In a large glass measuring cup or bowl, mix the teff flour, yeast, and 2 cups of water. Cover loosely with plastic wrap, and set aside for 36 to 48 hours to ferment. Begin tasting the batter for sourness at about 36 hours.

2. Add the flour blend, salt, and baking soda to the fermented teff mixture, stirring to mix. Add the remaining 1 cup of water a little at a time, just until the batter is pourable but thinner than a pancake batter.

3. Heat a 10- or 12-inch skillet over medium heat. Pour ¼ to ⅓ cup of batter into the center of the skillet and immediately tilt to coat the skillet. If it does not easily spread, add a little bit of water.

4. Cook for 1 minute, then cover the skillet and cook for another minute. The injera should easily lift from the pan with a spatula. Transfer the cooked injera to a cooling rack.

5. Repeat with the remaining batter. Meanwhile, transfer each cooked injera onto the cooling rack, placing a sheet of parchment paper between each of the breads.

INGREDIENT TIP: You can use a commercial gluten-free flour blend in place of the White Bread Flour Blend if you wish.

chapter nine
Quick Breads

chocolate-zucchini bread

PREP TIME: 10 minutes · **COOK TIME:** 50 minutes

This decadent quick bread hides mounds of shredded zucchini in a rich, chocolate loaf cake. If you don't feel like telling anyone the hidden ingredient, your secret is safe with me.

MAKES 1 LOAF

TOOLS

- 9-by-5-inch loaf pan
- Parchment paper

10 tablespoons (1¼ sticks) plus 2 teaspoons butter or nondairy butter, at room temperature

1 cup brown sugar

1 tablespoon vanilla extract

2 eggs, at room temperature

1 cup Multigrain Flour Blend (page 10)

½ cup unsweetened cocoa powder

2 teaspoons double-acting, aluminum-free, gluten-free baking powder

1 teaspoon sea salt

½ teaspoon xanthan gum

2 cups loosely packed shredded zucchini

1. Preheat the oven to 350°F. Line a 9-by-5-inch loaf pan with parchment paper.

2. In a large mixing bowl, cream the butter and sugar, beating until light and fluffy, about 1 minute.

3. Add the vanilla and eggs. Beat until thoroughly mixed, about 30 seconds.

4. In a separate bowl, sift the flour blend, cocoa powder, baking powder, salt, and xanthan gum. Add the flour mixture to the butter-egg mixture, and mix until just blended.

5. Wring the zucchini with your hands to squeeze out some of the excess water. Fold the zucchini into the batter.

6. Pour the batter into the prepared pan.

7. Bake for 45 to 50 minutes, until a wooden skewer inserted in the center of the loaf comes out clean.

INGREDIENT TIP: Use the best-quality cocoa powder you can— it really does make a difference here.

pumpkin bread

PREP TIME: 10 minutes • **COOK TIME:** 45 minutes

Dense, sweet, and brimming with the flavors of fall, pumpkin bread is one of my favorite quick breads, but it took me years to craft a gluten-free version that lived up to my high expectations. In this recipe, I use extra-virgin olive oil because it complements the flavor of winter squashes, like pumpkin. To me, the texture and flavor of this treat are perfect, with just the right amount of pumpkin and spices.

MAKES 1 LOAF

TOOLS

- 9-by-5-inch loaf pan
- Parchment paper

1 cup garbanzo bean flour

1 cup unpacked brown sugar

½ cup potato starch

¼ cup white rice flour

2 tablespoons pumpkin pie spice

2¾ teaspoons double-acting, aluminum-free, gluten-free baking powder

¾ teaspoon sea salt

¼ teaspoon xanthan gum

½ cup extra-virgin olive oil

1 cup pumpkin purée

¾ cup hot water

½ tablespoon apple cider vinegar

½ cup raisins (optional)

1. Preheat the oven to 325°F. Line a 9-inch-by-5-inch loaf pan with parchment paper.

2. In a medium bowl, mix together the garbanzo bean flour, brown sugar, potato starch, white rice flour, pumpkin pie spice, baking powder, salt, and xanthan gum.

3. Add the oil and pumpkin purée, and stir until just combined.

4. Add the hot water and vinegar, and stir until blended.

5. Fold in the raisins (if using).

6. Scrape the batter into the prepared pan and place it on the center rack of the oven. Bake for 40 to 45 minutes. Allow to rest in the pan for at least 30 minutes before slicing and serving.

BAKING TIP: Resist the temptation to use an entire can of pumpkin purée. Too much will yield a bread with the texture of pie filling.

apple-cinnamon bread

PREP TIME: 10 minutes • **COOK TIME:** 1 hour 15 minutes

This recipe is adapted from Erin McKenna's apple-cinnamon toastie in her book *Babycakes*, but my version has a lot less sugar and streamlines the baking process for a quick and easy bread that's sure to brighten your fall mornings.

MAKES 1 LOAF

TOOLS

- Shallow baking dish
- 9-by-5-inch loaf pan
- Parchment paper

4 Granny Smith apples, peeled, cored, and cut into 1-inch pieces

1 tablespoon freshly squeezed lemon juice

1 tablespoon sugar

1 teaspoon ground cinnamon

1 cup garbanzo bean flour

¾ cup unpacked brown sugar

½ cup potato starch

¼ cup white rice flour

1 tablespoon ground cinnamon

2¾ teaspoons double-acting, aluminum-free, gluten-free baking powder

¾ teaspoon sea salt

½ teaspoon xanthan gum

1 cup unsweetened applesauce

½ cup canola oil

½ cup water

½ tablespoon apple cider vinegar

1. Preheat the oven to 400°F. In a shallow baking dish, toss the apples, lemon juice, sugar, and cinnamon. Roast for 30 minutes, or until tender.

2. Reduce the oven temperature to 325°F. Line a 9-by-5-inch loaf pan with parchment paper.

3. In a medium bowl, mix the garbanzo bean flour, brown sugar, potato starch, white rice flour, cinnamon, baking powder, salt, and xanthan gum.

4. Add the applesauce and oil, and stir until just combined.

5. Add the water and vinegar, and stir until blended.

6. Fold in the roasted apples.

7. Pour the batter into the prepared loaf pan, and place it on the center rack of the oven. Bake for 45 minutes. Allow to rest in the pan for at least 30 minutes before slicing and serving.

INGREDIENT TIP: To measure the brown sugar, dip your measuring cup into the sugar to scoop, but do not pack it.

morning glory muffins

PREP TIME: 10 minutes • **COOK TIME:** 20 minutes

I love packing morning glory muffins in my kids' school lunch boxes, because I know that if they eat nothing else, they're still getting a healthy dose of gluten-free whole grains, carrots, apples, raisins, and walnuts. To reduce the sugar, you can use just ¼ cup. They won't be as sweet, of course, but they will be a touch healthier. My kids sometimes accuse me of depriving them of sugar, so I use half a cup, but do what seems best to you.

MAKES 12 MUFFINS

TOOLS

- 12-cup muffin tin
- Paper muffin liners

1⅓ cups Multigrain Flour Blend (page 10)

1 teaspoon baking soda

1 teaspoon ground cinnamon

½ teaspoon sea salt

2 eggs

½ cup unsweetened applesauce

½ cup brown sugar

⅓ cup canola oil

1 carrot, shredded

1 small apple, peeled, cored, and diced

½ cup raisins

½ cup finely chopped walnuts (optional)

1. Preheat the oven to 375°F. Line a 12-cup muffin tin with paper liners.

2. In a large bowl, mix the flour blend with the baking soda, cinnamon, and salt.

3. In a separate bowl, whisk together the eggs, applesauce, brown sugar, and oil. Add the egg mixture to the flour blend mixture and stir until just combined. Fold in the carrot, apple, raisins, and walnuts (if using).

4. Divide the batter between the muffin cups, and bake for 15 to 18 minutes, until golden brown and puffy. Allow to cool for 5 minutes before removing from the muffin tin.

SUBSTITUTION TIP: Turn these into tiny carrot cakes by omitting the apple. Replace the apple with one additional carrot. Whisk up a quick cream cheese frosting with 4 ounces cream cheese, 1 cup powdered sugar, and 1 teaspoon vanilla extract.

coffee cake

PREP TIME: 5 minutes · **COOK TIME:** 25 minutes

Before going gluten-free, I loved Starbucks' coffee cake. It paired perfectly with a steaming cup of coffee on Saturday mornings. This version has all of the airy lightness of the cake and crispy topping without the gluten hangover of the traditional version. Even better, I've snuck in a few whole-grain flours for a blend that's 75 percent whole grain! Enjoy this coffee cake with a few fried eggs and a slice of bacon for a yummy brunch.

SERVES 9

TOOLS

- 8-by-8-inch baking dish

Butter or shortening, for greasing

2 cups Multigrain Flour Blend (page 10)

½ teaspoon xanthan gum

¾ cup brown sugar, divided

2½ teaspoons double-acting, aluminum-free, gluten-free baking powder

2 teaspoons ground cinnamon, divided

½ teaspoon sea salt, plus a pinch

½ cup milk or nondairy milk

1 egg

6 tablespoons (¾ stick) melted butter or oil, divided, plus more for greasing

1 teaspoon vanilla extract

1. Preheat the oven to 350°F. Grease the interior of an 8-by-8-inch baking dish with butter or shortening.

2. In a large bowl, mix the flour blend and xanthan gum. Reserve ½ cup of the flour mixture and set aside.

3. Add ½ cup of brown sugar, the baking powder, 1 teaspoon of ground cinnamon, and ½ teaspoon salt to the flour mixture in the large bowl, and stir to mix. Make a well in the center of the ingredients.

4. Add the milk, egg, 2 tablespoons of butter, and vanilla. Stir until no lumps remain, then pour the batter into the prepared baking dish.

5. In a separate bowl, mix the reserved flour mixture with the remaining ¼ cup brown sugar, remaining 1 teaspoon cinnamon, remaining pinch of salt, and remaining 4 tablespoons of butter. Use your hands to combine the mixture until it resembles coarse crumbs. Sprinkle the crumbs over the cake.

6. Bake for 25 minutes, or until a cake tester comes out clean. Allow to cool completely before slicing and serving.

INGREDIENT TIP: Mix this gluten-free flour blend ahead of time and store in a covered container so this cake is ready to whip up at a moment's notice.

irish soda bread

PREP TIME: 5 minutes • **COOK TIME:** 40 minutes

I was tempted to put this bread into the Artisan Breads chapter, because it is not a sweet bread like most of the other quick breads in this chapter. However, because it is leavened with baking powder and soda, it's well placed here. This bread is good for toasting, making crostini, or serving with dinner.

MAKES 1 LOAF

TOOLS

- 8-inch round cake pan
- Food processor

1 teaspoon canola oil

1 tablespoon brown rice flour

2 cups Multigrain Flour Blend (page 10)

5 tablespoons sugar, divided

1½ teaspoons double-acting, aluminum-free, gluten-free baking powder

1 teaspoon sea salt

¾ teaspoon xanthan gum

¾ teaspoon baking soda

4 tablespoons cold butter, cut into pieces

1 cup buttermilk

⅔ cup raisins

1. Preheat the oven to 375°F. Coat an 8-inch round cake pan with the oil, then sprinkle with the brown rice flour. Shake out any excess.

2. In a food processor, add the flour blend, 4 tablespoons of sugar, the baking powder, salt, xanthan gum, and baking soda. Pulse a few times just to combine.

3. Add the butter and pulse until somewhat blended, with small chunks of butter remaining.

4. Stir in the buttermilk and raisins.

5. Transfer the dough to the prepared pan, and sprinkle with the remaining 1 tablespoon of sugar.

6. Bake for 40 minutes, until a cake tester comes out clean. Allow to cool completely before slicing.

VARIATION TIP: For a dairy-free version, use a dairy-free butter substitute, such as Earth Balance Buttery Spread, and replace the buttermilk with 1 cup unsweetened almond milk mixed with 1 teaspoon apple cider vinegar or lemon juice.

cornbread

PREP TIME: 5 minutes • **COOK TIME:** 25 minutes

Some breads are essential to my gluten-free recipe box not only because they're just plain good but also because they are indispensable to other meals. In the case of cornbread, I can honestly say that I believe chili is incomplete without it. Add a little honey and butter, and you have a little slice of heaven.

SERVES 9

TOOLS

- 8-by-8-inch baking dish

Butter or shortening, for greasing

1 cup Multigrain Flour Blend (page 10)

1 cup finely ground cornmeal

2 tablespoons sugar

2½ teaspoons double-acting, aluminum-free, gluten-free baking powder

1 teaspoon sea salt

¾ teaspoon xanthan gum

2 eggs

¾ cup milk or nondairy milk

4 tablespoons butter or nondairy butter, melted

1 cup frozen corn kernels

1. Preheat the oven to 350°F. Grease the interior of an 8-inch-by-8-inch baking dish with butter or shortening.

2. In a large bowl, mix the flour blend, cornmeal, sugar, baking powder, salt, and xanthan gum.

3. Add the eggs, milk, and melted butter. Stir until no lumps remain.

4. Fold in the corn kernels, then pour the batter into the prepared baking dish.

5. Bake for 25 minutes, or until a cake tester comes out clean. Allow to cool completely before slicing and serving.

INGREDIENT TIP: Cornmeal varieties sold in the grocery store can have vastly different consistencies. Some varieties are gritty, like polenta, while others are as fine as all-purpose flour. In this cornbread, I use a finely ground cornmeal.

blueberry-lemon scones

PREP TIME: 5 minutes · **COOK TIME:** 15 minutes

I lived in England for the better part of a year and sadly never enjoyed scones, because none were gluten-free. It's about five years late, but it's time to have my scones and eat them too! Jazz things up by folding in currants, dried cranberries, and orange zest, or even white chocolate chips and a handful of fresh raspberries.

MAKES 8 SCONES

TOOLS

- Food processor
- Baking sheet

1¾ cups Multigrain Flour Blend (page 10), plus more for dusting

¼ cup sugar, plus 1 tablespoon

2½ teaspoons double-acting, aluminum-free, gluten-free baking powder

½ teaspoon sea salt

4 tablespoons cold butter or nondairy butter, cut into pieces

2 eggs

⅓ cup heavy cream or nondairy cream

1 teaspoon vanilla extract

1 cup fresh blueberries

1 teaspoon grated lemon zest

1. Preheat the oven to 425°F.

2. In a food processor, combine the flour blend, ¼ cup of sugar, baking powder, and salt. Pulse one or two times just to integrate.

3. Add the cold butter and pulse until the mixture almost resembles coarse sand.

4. Add the eggs, heavy cream, and vanilla, and blend for a few seconds, just until integrated. Fold in the blueberries and lemon zest.

5. Dust a clean work surface with flour blend and gently roll out the dough to a 1-inch thickness. Cut into wedges and place on a baking sheet.

6. Sprinkle the remaining 1 tablespoon of sugar over the scones.

7. Bake for 15 minutes, until lightly browned.

SUBSTITUTION TIP: Fresh raspberries or ½ cup of dried fruit, such as currants, cranberries, cherries, or candied citrus, works well here in place of the blueberries.

green chile and cheddar scones

PREP TIME: 5 minutes · **COOK TIME:** 15 minutes

When you want something a little heftier to go with your chili or corn chowder, opt for these dense and crumbly green chile and cheddar scones. The spicy green chile gives the scones a nice kick, while the cheddar adds a savory richness.

MAKES 8 SCONES

TOOLS

- Food processor
- Baking sheet
- Parchment paper

1¾ cups Multigrain Flour Blend (page 10), plus more for dusting

1 tablespoon sugar

2½ teaspoons double-acting, aluminum-free, gluten-free baking powder

½ teaspoon sea salt

4 tablespoons cold butter or nondairy butter, cut into pieces

2 eggs

⅓ cup heavy cream or nondairy cream

½ cup shredded sharp cheddar cheese

¼ cup canned green chiles, drained

1. Preheat the oven to 425°F.

2. In a food processor, combine the flour blend, sugar, baking powder, and salt. Pulse one or two times just to integrate.

3. Add the cold butter and pulse until the mixture almost resembles coarse sand.

4. Add the eggs and heavy cream, and blend for a few seconds, just until integrated.

5. Fold in the cheese and chiles.

6. Dust a clean work surface with flour blend and roll out the dough to a 1-inch thickness. Cut into wedges and place on a baking sheet lined with parchment paper. Bake for 15 minutes, until lightly browned.

SUBSTITUTION TIP: For dairy-free scones, use nondairy butter and cream, and fold in vegan cheddar cheese shreds.

shortbread

PREP TIME: 10 minutes • **COOK TIME:** 40 minutes

Although it has *bread* in its name, shortbread is more like a rich, barely sweet butter cookie. But, if bread is healthy and cookies are not, let's just call it bread, shall we? Variations for shortbread involve dipping in melted chocolate, and that's lovely, but I prefer the straightforward, simple shortbread, which lets the flavor of good butter shine through.

MAKES 9 COOKIES

TOOLS

- 8-by-8-inch baking dish
- Parchment paper

8 tablespoons (1 stick) unsalted butter, at room temperature

⅓ cup sugar

2 teaspoons vanilla extract

1 egg yolk

1¼ cups Multigrain Flour Blend (page 10)

1¼ teaspoons sea salt

¼ teaspoon xanthan gum

1. Preheat the oven to 325°F. Line an 8-by-8-inch baking dish with parchment paper.

2. In a large bowl, combine the butter and sugar, and mix until creamed, about 1 minute.

3. Add the vanilla and egg yolk, and beat until emulsified.

4. Into a separate bowl, sift the flour blend, salt, and xanthan gum. Add the flour mixture to the butter-sugar mixture, and mix until thoroughly integrated.

5. Spread the mixture into the prepared baking dish. Prick all over with a fork. Bake for 5 minutes, then reduce the heat to 300°F and bake for another 35 minutes, or until the shortbread is barely golden. Remove from the oven and allow to cool completely before cutting into 9 squares.

INGREDIENT TIP: Opt for a good-quality organic, grass-fed butter if you can. It really does make a difference.

VARIATION TIP: For a dairy-free version, you can also use a non-dairy butter substitute, such as Earth Balance Buttery Spread, but because the flavor of the butter is so integral to the recipe, it will not brown the same way or have the same flavor that the butterfat provides.

cherry poppy seed bread

PREP TIME: 10 minutes • **COOK TIME:** 45 minutes

This is the kind of bread that you would order at a coffee shop in Portland, Oregon, and enjoy with a cup of French press coffee. I grew up enjoying locally grown hazelnuts, and both the city and its regional ingredients have a special place in my heart.

MAKES 1 LOAF

TOOLS

- 9-by-5-inch loaf pan
- Parchment paper

5 tablespoons plus 1 teaspoon butter or nondairy butter, at room temperature

¼ cup brown sugar

2 eggs, at room temperature

1 teaspoon vanilla extract

2 cups almond flour (not almond meal)

1 teaspoon double-acting, aluminum-free, gluten-free baking powder

½ teaspoon sea salt

2 cups toasted hazelnuts

1 cup dried cherries

2 tablespoons poppy seeds

1. Preheat the oven to 350°F. Line a 9-by-5-inch loaf pan with parchment paper.

2. In a large bowl, combine the butter and sugar, and mix until creamed, about 1 minute.

3. Add the eggs and vanilla. Beat until emulsified, about 30 seconds.

4. Stir in the almond flour, baking powder, and salt until just integrated. Fold in the hazelnuts, cherries, and poppy seeds.

5. Spoon the mixture into the prepared pan.

6. Bake for 40 to 45 minutes, until the top is golden and a wooden skewer inserted in the center comes out clean.

VARIATION TIP: If you want to vary the nuts and seeds in this bread, try dried cranberries, roughly chopped dried apricots, raisins, walnuts, pecans, macadamia nuts, or roughly chopped roasted almonds.

norwegian nut and seed bread

PREP TIME: 10 minutes • **COOK TIME:** 45 minutes

This bread has an unassuming rustic quality (that I adore) without being austere. It is naturally grain-free and made with nuts, seeds, eggs, and oil for a rich, dense, and crumbly texture.

MAKES 1 LOAF

TOOLS

- 9-by-5-inch loaf pan
- Parchment paper

⅔ cup sunflower seeds

⅔ cup toasted hazelnuts

⅔ cup walnuts

⅔ cup toasted almonds

⅔ cup pumpkin seeds

¼ cup poppy seeds or sesame seeds

5 eggs, at room temperature

½ cup olive oil (does not need to be extra-virgin)

1½ teaspoons sea salt

1 teaspoon vanilla extract

1. Preheat the oven to 325°F. Line a 9-by-5-inch loaf pan with parchment paper.

2. In a large bowl, stir together the sunflower seeds, hazelnuts, walnuts, almonds, pumpkin seeds, and poppy seeds. Mix in the eggs, oil, salt, and vanilla.

3. Spoon the mixture into the prepared pan.

4. Bake for 40 to 45 minutes, until the top is golden and a wooden skewer inserted in the center comes out clean.

INGREDIENT TIP: If you purchase raw hazelnuts, toast them on a rimmed baking sheet in the oven at 275°F for 15 to 20 minutes, shaking the pan one or twice during the baking time. Be very careful not to scorch them! Place the warm hazelnuts between 2 clean kitchen towels and rub gently to remove the papery skins.

chapter ten
Sweet Breads

stollen

PREP TIME: 15 minutes, plus 1 hour to prepare the sponge and 45 minutes to rise
COOK TIME: 40 minutes

My husband grew up in Germany and brought many holiday traditions into our relationship. One of my favorites is *Christollen*, a fruit-studded yeast bread filled with sweet marzipan and topped with a thick layer of powdered sugar. It is naturally somewhat dry, crumbly, and heavy, making the adaptation to gluten-free baking surprisingly easy. Be sure to read the entire recipe before starting. It includes making a sponge, which takes an extra hour, but this brings out flavor in the finished bread.

MAKES 1 LOAF

TOOLS

- Plastic wrap
- 6-by-10-inch baking dish
- Parchment paper

½ cup candied citrus peel

½ cup raisins or dried cranberries

½ cup brandy

1 cup brown rice flour

¼ cup plus 2 tablespoons potato starch

2 tablespoons tapioca starch

½ cup whole milk or nondairy milk, warmed to 110°F

1 (¼-ounce) packet active dry yeast

¾ teaspoon xanthan gum

½ tablespoon sugar

½ teaspoon sea salt

½ teaspoon ground cinnamon

1 egg, at room temperature

2½ tablespoons butter or nondairy butter, at room temperature

Zest of 1 lemon

Zest of 1 orange

2 ounces marzipan

Vegetable oil, for brushing

Powdered sugar

1. Combine the candied citrus peel, raisins, and brandy in a nonreactive dish to soak. Set aside.

2. In a large bowl, sift together the brown rice flour, potato starch, and tapioca starch.

3. To make the sponge, transfer ½ cup of the flour mixture to a large glass measuring cup or another nonreactive dish. Add the warmed milk and yeast. Whisk to blend. Cover the sponge with plastic wrap and set aside for 1 hour.

4. To the large bowl with the remaining flour mixture, add the xanthan gum, sugar, salt, and cinnamon.

5. Add the sponge, egg, butter, lemon zest, and orange zest. Beat for 30 seconds. Scrape down the sides of the bowl, and mix for 3 minutes.

6. Line a 6-by-10-inch baking dish with parchment paper.

7. Place slightly more than half of the dough into the dish and spread it to the edges.

8. Cut the marzipan into rectangles and lay them down the center of the dough. The row of marzipan should be about 3 inches wide by 8 inches long.

9. Top the marzipan with the remaining bread dough, mounding it up in the center to form a tall log shape, though it will not be perfectly round.

10. Allow to rise at room temperature for about 45 minutes. It will rise by about 50 percent but not double in size.

11. Preheat the oven to 350°F. Bake for 40 minutes until the bread is deeply browned. It should register 190°F in the center of the loaf.

12. Immediately brush the bread with oil, and use a fine-mesh sieve to sift powdered sugar over the top. Wait 5 minutes and repeat the application of powdered sugar.

INGREDIENT TIP: To make your own candied citrus peel, place 1 cup lemon, orange, and grapefruit peel cut into ¼-inch-wide slices into a pot of boiling water. Cook for 10 minutes, then drain. Bring 1 cup sugar and 1 cup water to a simmer, stirring to dissolve the sugar. Cook the citrus peel in the sugar water for 10 more minutes. Strain, reserving the cooking liquid, and transfer the citrus peel to a mesh cooling rack. You can use the reserved liquid to add a hint of sweetness to salad dressings or sparkling water. You can also use it to make your own *glühwein*, a German mulled wine—it works well because you don't have to cook the wine to dissolve the sugar.

apple kuchen

PREP TIME: 15 minutes, plus 45 minutes to rise • **COOK TIME:** 25 minutes

Apple kuchen—or apple cake—is a German yeast bread topped with diced apples, toasted almonds, and a simple powdered sugar glaze. It uses a similar dough to the Cinnamon Rolls (page 113) but requires no futzing about with rolling the dough.

SERVES 8

TOOLS

- Springform pan

For the glaze

½ cup powdered sugar

1 tablespoon milk or nondairy milk

For the cake

5 tablespoons butter or nondairy butter, at room temperature, divided

2 cups plus 1 tablespoon White Bread Flour Blend (page 10), divided

½ cup milk or nondairy milk, warmed to 110°F

1 (¼-ounce) packet active dry yeast

3 tablespoons sugar

1 teaspoon xanthan gum

¾ teaspoon sea salt

3 eggs, at room temperature, divided

1 teaspoon vanilla extract

2 tablespoons heavy cream or nondairy cream

2 apples, peeled, cored, and finely diced

2 tablespoons toasted sliced almonds

To make the glaze

In a small bowl, whisk together the powdered sugar and milk. Set aside.

To make the cake

1. Coat the interior of a springform pan with 1 tablespoon of butter, and dust with 1 tablespoon of flour blend. Set aside.

2. In a small bowl, mix together ¼ cup of flour blend with the warm milk and yeast.

3. In a large bowl, mix together the remaining 1¾ cups of flour blend, sugar, xanthan gum, and salt.

4. Add the yeast-milk mixture to the bowl, along with the remaining 4 tablespoons of butter, 2 eggs, and vanilla. Mix for 15 seconds. Scrape down the sides of the bowl with a spatula. Mix for an additional 3 minutes.

5. Transfer the dough to the prepared pan. Allow the dough to rise for 45 minutes, until puffy. Meanwhile, preheat the oven to 375°F.

6. In a small bowl, whisk the cream and the remaining egg until thoroughly blended. Pour the mixture over the risen dough. Gently sprinkle the apples and almonds on top.

7. Bake for 22 to 25 minutes, until the top is golden brown and the center is set.

8. Drizzle the glaze over the cooked apple kuchen. Allow to rest for at least 30 minutes before serving.

INGREDIENT TIP: To reduce the sugar, simply omit the powdered sugar glaze and add 1 tablespoon brown sugar to the cream-egg mixture.

brioche

PREP TIME: 10 minutes, plus 1 hour to prepare the sponge • **COOK TIME:** 20 minutes

Traditional brioche is made with a heart-stopping amount of butter and eggs, which yields rich, gorgeously puffed loaves with a delicate, tender crumb. This gluten-free version is no different, although the top will not have the classic brioche dome shape. Nevertheless, the flavor is superb and will keep you reaching for second helpings.

MAKES 6 (4-INCH) BRIOCHE

TOOLS

- 6 brioche molds
- Plastic wrap
- Rimmed baking sheet

10 tablespoons (1¼ sticks) butter or nondairy butter, at room temperature, divided

2 cups plus 2 tablespoons White Bread Flour Blend (page 10), divided

3 tablespoons sugar, divided

½ cup milk or nondairy milk, warmed to 110°F

1 (¼-ounce) packet active dry yeast

1 teaspoon xanthan gum

¾ teaspoon sea salt

3 eggs, at room temperature

1. Coat the insides of the brioche molds with 2 tablespoons of butter and sprinkle with 2 tablespoons of flour blend. Set aside.

2. Place ½ cup of flour blend in a large glass measuring cup or another nonreactive dish. Add 1 tablespoon of sugar, warmed milk, and yeast, and whisk to blend. Cover with plastic wrap and set aside for 1 hour to form a sponge.

3. In a large bowl, combine the remaining 1½ cups of flour blend, the remaining 2 tablespoons of sugar, xanthan gum, and salt. Add the sponge, the remaining 8 tablespoons of butter, and eggs. Mix for 15 seconds. Scrape down the sides of the bowl. Mix for 3 additional minutes.

4. Divide the dough between the molds. Set the molds on a rimmed baking sheet and allow the dough to rise for 1 hour.

5. Preheat the oven to 350°F.

6. Bake the brioche for 17 to 19 minutes, until golden brown and puffy.

7. Allow to rest for 15 minutes before serving.

INGREDIENT TIP: To quickly warm eggs to room temperature, place them in a bowl of warm (but not hot) water for 15 minutes.

croissants

PREP TIME: 1 hour plus 11 hours to chill • **COOK TIME:** 45 minutes

To craft these exquisite pastries, I began with an excellent traditional croissant recipe. Working with the gluten-free dough required a little more patience—it is somewhat sticky— but the final result exceeded my expectations. The croissants are tender, buttery, and beautifully browned. Even better, the dough feels alive and soft in your hands as you roll it out.

MAKES 20 CROISSANTS

TOOLS

- Stand mixer (optional)
- Parchment paper
- Plastic wrap
- Baking dish
- 2 baking sheets

For the butter block

2 tablespoons White Bread Flour Blend (page 10)

1 cup (2 sticks) unsalted butter, barely softened (see Ingredient tip)

For the croissants

3⅓ cups White Bread Flour Blend (page 10), plus more for dusting

2 tablespoons sugar

1 (¼-ounce) packet active dry yeast

2 teaspoons xanthan gum

1½ teaspoons sea salt

1 tablespoon butter, melted, plus more for greasing

1¼ cups 2 percent milk, warmed to 110°F

1 egg

1 tablespoon water

To make the butter block

1. In a large bowl or the bowl of a stand mixer fitted with the paddle attachment, combine the flour blend and butter. Mix until well blended, about 2 minutes, scraping the butter away from the paddle (if using) as needed.

2. Place the butter block onto a large sheet of parchment paper, and shape into a rectangle about 5 inches by 7 inches. Fold the parchment over it to seal. Place in the refrigerator for 1 hour, or until firm but pliable enough to make an indentation by pressing with your fingertip.

To make the croissants

1. Clean the bowl, then combine the flour blend, sugar, yeast, xanthan gum, and salt. Add the melted butter and warm milk, and mix for 15 seconds by hand or with the paddle attachment. Scrape down the sides of the bowl. Mix for 3 additional minutes.

2. Lightly grease another large bowl with butter, and transfer the dough into it. Place the bowl in the refrigerator for 2 hours.

3. Remove the dough and the butter block from the refrigerator.

4. Lightly dust a large sheet of parchment paper with flour blend. Roll the dough into a rectangle about 8 inches by 11 inches, with the shorter side facing you. Place the butter block onto the dough along the side closest to you (figure A). (The 7-inch side of the butter block should be next to the 8-inch side of the dough.) Fold the remaining half of the dough over the butter block (figure B), and gently seal it along the edges (figure C).

5. Dust the dough with flour blend to prevent the rolling pin from sticking.

Figure A

Figure B

Figure C

Figure D

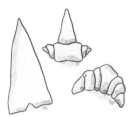
Figure E

6. Roll the dough with the butter block inside it, until it is again about 8 inches by 11 inches.

7. Fold the dough into thirds, as if folding a business letter.

8. Again, roll the dough out until it is roughly 8 inches by 11 inches.

9. Again, fold the dough as if folding a business letter. Wrap the dough tightly in plastic wrap and place in the refrigerator for 1 hour 30 minutes.

10. Repeat steps 3 through 9, but refrigerate the dough overnight.

11. Preheat the oven to 300°F for 1 minute until it reaches 80°F. Turn off the oven. Place a baking dish containing 2 cups of hot water on the bottom rack. Line 2 baking sheets with parchment paper and set aside.

12. Remove the dough from the refrigerator, divide it into 2 portions, and return 1 portion, wrapped tightly in plastic wrap, to the refrigerator.

13. Place a large, clean sheet of parchment paper on the work surface. Dust it lightly with flour blend to prevent the croissant dough from sticking.

14. Roll the dough out into a large rectangle until it is less than ¼ inch thick. Make sure it does not stick to the parchment paper by turning the dough, or even flipping it once, before it is fully rolled out.

15. Divide the rectangle into 2 narrow rectangles. Use a sharp knife or pizza wheel to cut these into triangles (figure D).

16. One at a time, carefully lift each triangle from the parchment and roll it loosely, starting at the bottom and rolling toward the point. Gently curve the ends of the roll into a crescent shape and place the dough onto a prepared baking sheet (figure E). The tip of the dough (what was once the top of the triangle) should fold over the top of the croissant down toward the baking sheet but should not be tucked under.

CONTINUED ➤

17. Repeat with the remaining dough to fill 1 baking sheet. Place in the warmed oven to rise for 2 hours.

18. Remove the second block of dough from the refrigerator and repeat steps 11 through 17.

19. Remove both baking sheets from the oven and set them on the counter. Remove the baking dish with the steaming water.

20. Preheat the oven to 400°F.

21. In a small bowl, whisk the egg and water. Very gently brush the tops of the croissants with the egg wash. Place the first baking sheet on the middle rack in the oven and bake for 22 minutes, until the croissants are puffy and golden brown. Repeat with the second baking sheet.

22. Allow to cool completely before enjoying.

BAKING TIP: Avoid setting the baking sheets on top of the oven while it preheats. This will cause them to overproof.

INGREDIENT TIP: Allow cold butter to sit on the countertop for up to 30 minutes to let it soften slightly but not come up to room temperature.

almond croissants

PREP TIME: 1 hour plus 11 hours to chill · **COOK TIME:** 45 minutes

When I was in my early 20s, my favorite way to start the day was to stop by a café to pick up a cup of coffee and an almond croissant. These pastries are just like I remember them.

MAKES 20 CROISSANTS

TOOLS

- Stand mixer (optional)
- Parchment paper
- Plastic wrap
- Baking dish
- 2 baking sheets

For the butter block

2 tablespoons White Bread Flour Blend (page 10)

1 cup (2 sticks) unsalted butter, barely softened (see Ingredient tip)

For the croissants

3⅓ cups White Bread Flour Blend (page 10), plus more for dusting

2 tablespoons granulated sugar

1 (¼-ounce) packet active dry yeast

2 teaspoons xanthan gum

1½ teaspoons sea salt

1 tablespoon butter, melted, plus more for greasing

1¼ cups 2 percent milk, warmed to 110°F

8 ounces marzipan

1 egg

1 tablespoon water

½ cup thinly sliced toasted almonds

4 tablespoons powdered sugar

To make the butter block

1. In a large bowl or the bowl of a stand mixer fitted with the paddle attachment, combine the flour blend and butter. Mix until well blended, about 2 minutes, scraping the butter away from the paddle, if using, a few times as needed.

2. Place the butter block onto a large sheet of parchment paper and shape into a rectangle about 5 inches by 7 inches. Fold the parchment over it to seal. Place in the refrigerator for 1 hour, or until firm but pliable enough to make an indentation by pressing with your fingertip.

To make the croissants

1. Clean the bowl, then combine the flour blend, sugar, yeast, xanthan gum, and salt. Add the melted butter and warm milk, and mix for 15 seconds using the paddle attachment or by hand. Scrape down the sides of the bowl. Mix for 3 additional minutes.

2. Lightly grease another large bowl with butter, and transfer the dough into it. Place the bowl in the refrigerator for 2 hours.

3. Remove the dough and the butter block from the refrigerator.

4. Lightly dust a large sheet of parchment paper with flour blend. Roll the dough into a rectangle about 8 inches by 11 inches, with the shorter side facing you. Place the butter block onto the dough along the side closest to you. (The 7-inch side of the butter block should be next to the 8-inch side of the dough.) Fold the remaining half of the dough over the butter block and gently seal it along the edges.

5. Dust the dough with flour to prevent the rolling pin from sticking.

CONTINUED ➤

6. Roll the dough with the butter block inside it, until it is again about 8 inches by 11 inches.

7. Fold the dough into thirds as if folding a business letter.

8. Again, roll the dough out until it is roughly 8 inches by 11 inches.

9. Again, fold the dough as if folding a business letter. Wrap the dough tightly in plastic wrap and place in the refrigerator for 1 hour 30 minutes.

10. Repeat steps 3 through 9, but refrigerate the dough overnight.

11. Preheat the oven to 300°F for 1 minute until it reaches a temperature of 80°F. Turn off the oven. Place a baking dish containing 2 cups of hot water on the bottom rack of the oven. Line 2 baking sheets with parchment paper and set aside.

12. Remove the dough from the refrigerator, divide it into 2 portions, and return 1 portion, wrapped tightly in plastic wrap, to the refrigerator.

13. Place a large, clean sheet of parchment paper on the work surface. Dust it lightly with flour blend to prevent the croissant dough from sticking.

14. Roll the dough out into a large rectangle, until it is less than ¼ inch thick. Make sure it does not stick to the parchment paper by turning the dough, or even flipping it once, before it is fully rolled out.

15. Divide the rectangle into 2 narrow rectangles. Cut these into triangles using a sharp knife or a pizza wheel.

16. One at a time, carefully lift each triangle from the parchment. Place about 2 teaspoons of marzipan onto the bottom of the triangle, and roll it loosely, starting at the bottom and rolling toward the point. Gently curve the ends of the roll into a crescent shape, and place the dough onto a prepared baking sheet. The point of the dough should fold over the top of the croissant down toward the baking sheet, but should not be tucked under.

17. Repeat with the remaining dough to fill 1 baking sheet. Place in the warmed oven to rise for 2 hours.

18. Remove the second block of dough from the refrigerator, and repeat steps 11 through 17.

19. Remove both baking sheets from the oven and set them on the counter. Remove the baking dish with the steaming water.

20. Preheat the oven to 400°F.

21. In a small bowl, whisk together the egg and water. Very gently brush the tops of the croissants with the egg wash, and sprinkle with the almonds. Place the first baking sheet on the middle rack in the oven and bake for 22 minutes, until the croissants are puffy and golden brown. Immediately sift 1 tablespoon of powdered sugar over the top of all of the croissants.

22. Repeat step 21 with the second baking sheet.

23. Allow to cool completely before enjoying.

INGREDIENT TIP: Marzipan is made from ground blanched almonds and sugar. It can be purchased in a sealed container in the baking aisle.

INGREDIENT TIP: Allow cold butter to sit on the countertop for up to 30 minutes to let it soften slightly but not come up to room temperature.

pain au chocolat

PREP TIME: 1 hour plus 11 hours to chill · **COOK TIME:** 45 minutes

Filled with gooey dark chocolate, these pastries are a real treat. They remind me of all the fine pastries I enjoyed from coffee shops before going gluten-free.

MAKES 20 PASTRIES

TOOLS

- Stand mixer (optional)
- Parchment paper
- Plastic wrap
- Baking dish
- 2 baking sheets

For the butter block

2 tablespoons White Bread Flour Blend (page 10)

1 cup (2 sticks) unsalted butter, barely softened (see Ingredient tip)

For the pastries

3⅓ cups White Bread Flour Blend (page 10), plus more for dusting

2 tablespoons sugar

1 (¼-ounce) packet active dry yeast

2 teaspoons xanthan gum

1½ teaspoons sea salt

1 tablespoon butter, melted, plus more (not melted) for greasing

1¼ cups 2 percent milk, warmed to 110°F

1½ cups 60 percent cacao chocolate chips

1 egg

1 tablespoon water

To make the butter block

1. In a large bowl or the bowl of a stand mixer fitted with the paddle attachment, combine the flour blend and butter. Mix until well blended, about 2 minutes, scraping the butter away from the paddle, if using, as needed.

2. Place the butter block onto a large sheet of parchment paper and shape into a rectangle about 5 inches by 7 inches. Fold the parchment over it to seal. Place in the refrigerator for 1 hour, or until firm but pliable enough to make an indentation by pressing with your fingertip.

To make the pastries

1. Clean the bowl, then mix together the flour blend, sugar, yeast, xanthan gum, and salt. Add the melted butter and warm milk, and mix for 15 seconds using the paddle attachment or by hand. Scrape down the sides of the bowl. Mix for 3 additional minutes.

2. Lightly grease another large bowl with butter, and transfer the dough into it. Place the bowl in the refrigerator for 2 hours.

3. Remove the dough and the butter block from the refrigerator.

4. Lightly dust a large sheet of parchment paper with flour blend. Roll the dough into a rectangle about 8 inches by 11 inches, with the shorter side facing you. Place the butter block onto the dough along the side closest to you. (The 7-inch side of the butter block should be next to the 8-inch side of the dough.) Fold the remaining half of the dough over the butter block and gently seal it along the edges.

5. Dust the dough with flour to prevent the rolling pin from sticking.

6. Roll the dough with the butter block inside it, until it is again about 8 inches by 11 inches.

7. Fold the dough into thirds as if folding a business letter.

8. Again, roll the dough out until it is roughly 8 inches by 11 inches.

9. Again, fold the dough as if folding a business letter. Wrap the dough tightly in plastic wrap, and place in the refrigerator for 1 hour 30 minutes.

10. Repeat steps 3 through 9, but refrigerate the dough overnight.

11. Preheat the oven to 300°F for 1 minute until it reaches 80°F. Turn off the oven. Place a baking dish containing 2 cups of hot water on the bottom rack of the oven. Line 2 baking sheets with parchment paper and set aside.

12. Remove the dough from the refrigerator, divide it into 2 portions, and return 1 portion, wrapped tightly in plastic wrap, to the refrigerator.

13. Place a large, clean sheet of parchment paper onto the work surface. Dust it lightly with flour blend to prevent the dough from sticking.

14. Roll the dough out into a large rectangle until it is less than ¼ inch thick. Make sure it does not stick to the parchment paper by turning the dough, or even flipping it once, before it is fully rolled out.

15. Divide the rectangle into 2 narrow rectangles. Using a sharp knife or pizza wheel, cut these into a total of 10 rectangles.

CONTINUED ➤

16. Place 1 generous tablespoon of chocolate chips onto each rectangle and fold the dough tightly over the chocolate. Place the pastries onto 1 prepared baking sheet, and place in the warmed oven to rise for 2 hours.

17. Remove the second block of dough from the refrigerator, and repeat steps 11 through 16.

18. Remove both baking sheets from the oven and set them on the counter. Remove the baking dish with the steaming water.

19. Preheat the oven to 400°F.

20. In a small bowl, whisk together the egg and water. Very gently brush the tops of the pastries with the egg wash. Place the first baking sheet onto the middle rack in the oven and bake for 15 to 18 minutes, until the pastries are puffy and golden brown. Repeat with the second baking sheet.

21. Allow to cool completely before enjoying.

BAKING TIP: If you are having trouble sealing the pastries without smashing the dough, brush them gently with the egg wash before folding.

INGREDIENT TIP: Allow cold butter to sit on the countertop for up to 30 minutes to let it soften slightly but not come up to room temperature.

VARIATION TIP: This dough is also excellent for making savory pastries, such as salmon en croute or any other recipe requiring a puff pastry.

cinnamon rolls

PREP TIME: 15 minutes, plus 45 minutes to 1 hour to rise • **COOK TIME:** 25 minutes

My mom made cinnamon rolls every Christmas while I was growing up. The sweet treat became a distant memory when I left home and discovered I needed to follow a gluten-free diet. I didn't even attempt cinnamon rolls for years because they just seemed impossible. It was a challenge, but my White Bread Flour Blend proved the perfect solution, yielding tender, chewy cinnamon rolls with the perfect hint of sweetness.

MAKES 8 ROLLS

TOOLS

- 8-inch pie plate or cake pan
- Parchment paper

For the filling

¼ cup brown sugar

1 teaspoon ground cinnamon

For the glaze

½ cup powdered sugar

1 tablespoon milk or nondairy milk

For the rolls

2 cups White Bread Flour Blend (page 10), divided, plus more for dusting

½ cup milk or nondairy milk, warmed to 110°F

1 (¼-ounce) packet active dry yeast

¼ cup sugar

1 teaspoon xanthan gum

¾ teaspoon sea salt

3 tablespoons butter or nondairy butter, at room temperature, plus 1 tablespoon butter or nondairy butter, melted

2 eggs, at room temperature

To make the filling

In a small bowl, mix together the brown sugar and cinnamon. Set aside.

To make the glaze

In another small bowl, whisk together the powdered sugar and milk. Set aside.

To make the rolls

1. Line the interior of an 8-inch pie plate or cake pan with parchment paper. Set aside.

2. In a nonreactive dish, combine ¼ cup of flour blend with the warm milk and yeast.

3. In a large bowl, mix the remaining 1¾ cups flour blend, sugar, xanthan gum, and salt.

4. Add the yeast-milk mixture to the bowl along with the 3 tablespoons of butter and eggs. Mix for 15 seconds. Scrape down the sides of the bowl with a spatula. Mix for 3 additional minutes.

5. Line a clean work surface with parchment paper. Sprinkle generously with additional flour blend.

6. Transfer the dough from the mixer to the prepared work surface and spread into a rectangle about 6 inches by 10 inches; the long edge should be nearest to you.

CONTINUED ➤

cinnamon rolls CONTINUED

7. Brush the dough with the melted butter. Sprinkle the filling over the dough.

8. Lift one end of the parchment paper to help you roll the dough from one of the short ends to the other (across the work surface from left to right). It should easily release from the floured parchment. If parts of it stick, use a sharp knife to "peel" it from the parchment.

9. Roll the dough into the shape of a log. It will be somewhat flat. Use a clean knife to cut the dough into 2-inch rolls. Using the knife, transfer each roll into the prepared pan, nudging the dough into the desired round shape. Repeat with the remaining dough, scraping excess dough from the knife as needed.

10. Allow the dough to rise for 45 minutes to 1 hour, until very puffy. Preheat the oven to 375°F.

11. Bake for 20 to 22 minutes, until the tops are golden brown and the center is still somewhat soft.

12. Drizzle the glaze over the baked cinnamon rolls. Allow to rest for 10 to 15 minutes before serving.

BAKING TIP: A slower rise is better for these cinnamon rolls, so let them rise on the countertop instead of in a warmed oven, unless the ambient temperature in your home is well below 70°F.

popovers

PREP TIME: 10 minutes • **COOK TIME:** 25 minutes

Popovers are eggy breakfast buns that fall somewhere in between brioche and custard. They're leavened with ample eggs instead of yeast or chemical leaveners, making them a lovely addition to Passover festivities. Because a chewy texture is not so desirable in popovers, I opt for the Multigrain Flour Blend in this recipe. You can use a commercial flour blend instead, but if it contains xanthan or guar gum, omit the xanthan gum in this recipe.

MAKES 12 POPOVERS

TOOLS

- 12-cup popover pan or muffin tin (see Baking tip)

4 tablespoons butter or nondairy butter, melted, divided

1½ cups Multigrain Flour Blend (page 10)

1 tablespoon sugar

¼ teaspoon xanthan gum

⅛ teaspoon sea salt

3 eggs, at room temperature

1½ cups milk or nondairy milk, at room temperature

1. Preheat the oven to 425°F. Coat the interiors of the popover cups with 2 tablespoons of butter.

2. In a large bowl, whisk the flour blend, sugar, xanthan gum, and salt. Add the remaining 2 tablespoons of butter, eggs, and milk, and whisk until no lumps remain.

3. When the oven is preheated, place the prepared pan into it for 2 minutes. Remove the pan from the oven, and pour the mixture into the heated pan so each cup is about half full.

4. Bake for 25 minutes, until the popovers are gorgeously risen and browned.

BAKING TIP: A muffin tin is the most likely substitute for a proper popover pan, but it is not quite as deep and the walls of the cups are slanted, which affects the result. If you use a muffin tin, reduce the volume of ingredients by roughly one-third: Use 3 tablespoons butter, 1 cup flour blend, 2 teaspoons sugar, scant ¼ teaspoon xanthan gum, scant ⅛ teaspoon salt, 2 eggs, and 1 cup milk.

TROUBLESHOOTING TIP: Like other egg-leavened dishes, popovers require that you don't open the oven during baking.

Measurement Conversion Charts

VOLUME EQUIVALENTS (LIQUID)

US Standard	US Standard (ounces)	Metric (approx.)
2 tablespoons	1 fl. oz.	30 mL
¼ cup	2 fl. oz.	60 mL
½ cup	4 fl. oz.	120 mL
1 cup	8 fl. oz.	240 mL
1½ cups	12 fl. oz.	355 mL
2 cups or 1 pint	16 fl. oz.	475 mL
4 cups or 1 quart	32 fl. oz.	1 L
1 gallon	128 fl. oz.	4 L

OVEN TEMPERATURES

Fahrenheit	Celsius (approx.)
250°F	120°C
300°F	150°C
325°F	165°C
350°F	180°C
375°F	190°C
400°F	200°C
425°F	220°C
450°F	230°C

VOLUME EQUIVALENTS (DRY)

US Standard	Metric (approx.)
⅛ teaspoon	0.5 mL
¼ teaspoon	1 mL
½ teaspoon	2 mL
¾ teaspoon	4 mL
1 teaspoon	5 mL
1 tablespoon	15 mL
¼ cup	59 mL
⅓ cup	79 mL
½ cup	118 mL
⅔ cup	156 mL
¾ cup	177 mL
1 cup	235 mL
2 cups or 1 pint	475 mL
3 cups	700 mL
4 cups or 1 quart	1 L

WEIGHT EQUIVALENTS

US Standard	Metric (approx.)
½ ounce	15 g
1 ounce	30 g
2 ounces	60 g
4 ounces	115 g
8 ounces	225 g
12 ounces	340 g
16 ounces or 1 pound	455 g

References

Ellgen, Pamela. *The Gluten-Free Cookbook for Families*. Berkeley, CA: Rockridge Press, 2016.

Fisher, M.F.K. *The Art of Eating*. 50th anniversary ed. Boston: Houghton Mifflin Harcourt, 2004.

Flanner, Janet. *Paris Was Yesterday, 1925–1939*. Boston: Mariner Books, 1988.

Lawson, Nigella. *How to Be a Domestic Goddess*. New York: Hyperion, 2001.

McKenna, Erin. *Babycakes*. New York: Clarkson Potter, 2009.

Reinhart, Peter. *The Bread Baker's Apprentice*. Berkeley, CA: Ten Speed Press, 2001.

Roberts, Annalise G. *Gluten-Free Bread Baking Classics*, 2nd ed. Chicago: Surrey Books, 2008.

Resources

Celiac Disease Foundation, a nonprofit organization devoted to advocacy, education, and research:
Celiac.org

Beyond Celiac, an advocacy group for people with celiac disease:
BeyondCeliac.org

Bob's Red Mill:
BobsRedMill.com

Cultures for Health, natural products you make at home:
CulturesForHealth.com

King Arthur Flour:
KingArthurFlour.com

The Gluten-Free Cookbook for Families by Pamela Ellgen

Recipe Index

Index

Acknowledgments

While I was testing recipes for and writing this book, the Thomas Fire ravaged the coastal communities of Ventura and Santa Barbara, where I live. It was the largest fire in California's recorded history. I am forever grateful to the firefighters and first responders who kept our community safe and endured weeks away from their own families throughout the Christmas season.

Thank you to Rich, Brad, and Cole for your honest feedback throughout the recipe testing process and your patience as I spent long hours in the kitchen. I couldn't have done it without you.

As always, thank you to the amazing team at Callisto Media, who continually transforms my words and recipes into beautiful books that I'm proud to share with friends and family. Special thanks to Meg Ilasco, Elizabeth Castoria, and Patty Consolazio.

About the Author

PAMELA ELLGEN is a private chef, food writer, and cooking instructor in Santa Barbara, California. She specializes in gluten-free and plant-based cooking and is the author of the food blog *Surf Girl Eats*. She has written more than a dozen cookbooks, including *The Gluten-Free Cookbook for Families* and *The Big Dairy Free Cookbook*. Her work has been featured in *Outside* magazine, *Huffington Post*, *The Portland Tribune*, *Healthline*, *Livestrong*, and *The Nest*. When she's not in the kitchen, Pamela enjoys surfing and playing with her kids on the beach.

CPSIA information can be obtained
at www.ICGtesting.com
Printed in the USA
JSHW051901161021
19586JS00003B/3

9 781641 520195